JUST ANOTHER INDIAN

JUST ANOTHER INDIAN

A Serial Killer and Canada's Indifference

WARREN GOULDING

FIFTH
HOUSE

Cover design by Thinkinc, Calgary, Alberta.

Interior design by Articulate Eye, Saskatoon, Saskatchewan.

The publisher gratefully acknowledges the support of The Canada Council for the Arts and the Department of Canadian Heritage.

THE CANADA COUNCIL | LE CONSEIL DES ARTS
FOR THE ARTS | DU CANADA
SINCE 1957 | DEPUIS 1957

We acknowledge the financial support of the Government of Canada through the Book Publishing Industry Development Program for our publishing activities.

Printed in Canada.

06 07 08 09 / 9 8 7 6 5 4

CANADIAN CATALOGUING IN PUBLICATION DATA

Goulding, Warren David, 1950–

Just another Indian

ISBN 1–894004–51–5

1. Crawford, John Martin. 2. Serial murders—Canada—Case studies. 3. Murder—Canada—Public opinion. 4. Murder victims—Canada. 5. Indian women—Crimes against—Canada. I. Title.
HV6535.C3G68 2001   364.15'23'0971   C00-911175-1

Fifth House Ltd.
A Fitzhenry & Whiteside Company
1511-1800 4 Street SW
Calgary, Alberta, Canada
T2S 2S5

To my mother, Myrtle Goulding, whose love and encouragement have been a source of inspiration throughout my life.

This book is also dedicated to the memories of Shelley Napope, Calinda Waterhen, Eva Taysup, and Mary Jane Serloin. It is a tribute to the families they left behind. May they come to know that many Canadians share their sadness.

I hope that this book will honour the aboriginal peoples of Canada and shed light on the plight of the victims of a justice system that is anything but fair.

TABLE OF CONTENTS

ACKNOWLEDGEMENTS

Many people played vital roles in the production of *Just Another Indian: A Serial Killer and Canada's Indifference*.

I am grateful for having had the privilege of working with the enormously talented editor Donald Ward, who tackled the daunting task of transforming an aging journalist into something resembling an author. His good humour and intellect were much appreciated throughout this project.

Thanks also to JuVerna. "Kate," your sensitivity and discerning eye were an enormous help to me.

Many thanks to Fifth House Publishers and the folks at Fitzhenry & Whiteside for recognizing the importance of this story and the need for it to be told.

I am indebted to Dennis Berezowsky and the staff at the Court of Queen's Bench in Saskatoon, and Maurice Herauf, registrar at the Court of Queen's Bench in Regina.

Thanks to Mark Brayford, Terry Hinz, and Hugh Harradence for your openness and co-operation.

I appreciate the support of many friends, creditors, and other patient folk who were involved in the writing of this book. The list includes Cec Kanigan, Dr. Srini Chary, Ted and Tanyss Munro, and John Lagimodiere.

Special thanks to the families and friends of Shelley Napope, Eva Taysup, Calinda Waterhen, Mary Jane Serloin, and Shirley Lonethunder for assistance in what was a most difficult experience. I respect your desire to bring closure to these tragedies, and understand your need to allow the spirits of your daughters to find peace.

Finally, I am grateful for the support of the Saskatchewan Arts Board, without whose assistance this book could not have been written.

INTRODUCTION

Unlike many of the sordid characters with whom he shares the designation "serial killer," John Martin Crawford shuns publicity. He has staked his claim as one of the nation's most prolific sex killers with little fanfare. And indeed, in terms of self-preservation, Crawford could hardly have orchestrated a better scenario than his current situation. Housed in the Saskatchewan Penitentiary in Prince Albert, serving three concurrent life sentences, he is anonymous, his deeds virtually forgotten. Even within the confines of the P.A. Pen, an institution that has housed the likes of Clifford Olson and Charles Ng, few inmates are aware of Crawford or what he has done. His lack of celebrity bodes well for his survival. With a prison population that is 70 percent aboriginal, the unrepentant murderer doesn't need his fellow inmates to know of his predilection for killing young Native women.

As of this writing, Crawford has been convicted of four deaths, all of them women, all of them Native. He is also a suspect in at least three other murders or mysterious disappearances of aboriginal women in Saskatoon. But Crawford has been the beneficiary of a disinterested media and an equally impassive public. More important, his victims have suffered even further because of this indifference.

The first killing came in 1981 in Lethbridge, Alberta, when the then nineteen-year-old Crawford led Mary Jane Serloin to her death. The murder, coming just two days before Christmas, caused barely a ripple in the community. The Lethbridge *Herald* gave the story three column-inches in the second section, beneath a story about members of the local Kinette Club delivering 425 poinsettia plants to nursing homes and senior citizens lodges in the city. Two days later, the paper succinctly identified the victim whose "nude body was found in the alcove of the old No. 1 firehall." The story ran to forty-six words.

"It seems any time a Native is murdered," the victim's sister commented, "it isn't a major case. It's just another dead Indian."

Less than a decade later John Martin Crawford emerged from the penal system with an enhanced appetite for sex and mayhem. Fuelled by prescription and nonprescription drugs, alcohol, and solvents, he spent his evenings trolling for prostitutes and other women from whom he could obtain cheap sex. In 1990, while living in Saskatoon, he was fined for attempting to engage the services of a prostitute. Two years later he was charged with raping Janet Sylvestre, a thirty-six-year-old aboriginal woman. Before the year was up, he had murdered Shelley Napope, Eva Taysup, and Calinda Waterhen. At least, these are the women Crawford was convicted of killing when he finally came to trial in 1996. The naked body of Janet Sylvestre—the same woman he had allegedly raped—was discovered in a grove of trees near Saskatoon in October 1994. During the same period, two more women, Shirley Lonethunder and Cynthia Baldhead, ominously disappeared from the aboriginal community. If the police were suspicious that these women, too, had fallen into Crawford's murderous hands, they weren't saying, at least not publicly.

They didn't have to. No one was asking.

Law enforcement services had received reports of missing women and murdered women in and around Saskatoon for some time, but the police did not seem to take the disappearances of these women seriously—until bodies began turning up in a grove near the city. There were no posters soliciting information on the disappearances of Shelley Napope, Eva Taysup, Calinda Waterhen, or any of the dozens of Native women who are reported missing every year.

When Crawford appealed his conviction in January 1999, only one media outlet took any notice. A lone reporter from the Regina *LeaderPost* attended the half-day hearing in the Saskatchewan Court of Appeal in Regina, and was subsequently responsible for the account of the proceedings that made its way to the other papers in the Hollinger chain, including the Saskatoon *StarPhoenix*. None of the three television stations or half-dozen radio outlets in Saskatoon bothered to cover the story. Three months later, when Crawford's mother, Victoria, engaged the services of a Winnipeg law firm in an effort to get her son's case before the Supreme Court of Canada, nobody took any notice at all. When Crawford's leave to appeal was dismissed by the Supreme Court on March 30, 2000, hardly anyone noticed. The media had simply abandoned the story. Faced with increasing competition and diminishing resources, the media were struggling simply to meet the challenges of daily journalism in a diverse and demanding market. Crawford was yesterday's news. His victims and their families had had their moment in the spotlight. When the mainstream media did report on the story, many members of the Native community were offended by the coverage of Crawford's aboriginal victims. "Instead of thinking about these young women as individuals who had dreams, aspirations, hopes and people who loved them," wrote Janice Acoose in *Iskwewak: Neither Indian Princesses Nor Easy Squaws*, "we were encouraged to view them through stereotypical images."

In a column written at the time of the Crawford trial, Les MacPherson, a popular columnist with the Saskatoon *StarPhoenix*, asked why reporters from across Canada were not "climbing over each other to get at the story," and why it wasn't "generating anything like the publicity of . . . the Paul Bernardo trial." He determined that geography and a lack of compelling drama were responsible but that crying racism was an "almost entirely superficial" and "quite wrong" response. "Yes, the victims were Indian women, but that's largely by the way," he wrote.

MacPherson goes on to say that "more relevant than race is the nearly total absence of connections between the victims and the mainstream community. They inhabited an isolated underworld where people routinely drop in and out of sight." These women, he said, "did not maintain close contact with their immediate families. They were not expected home for dinner. Missing person reports were not outstanding on any of the three victims. Police were not beset by concerned family members demanding to know why not." Rather than condemning "white folks for not much caring about murdered Indian women," he asks, "who cared for them while they were still alive?"

In posing these questions, MacPherson is displaying a common ignorance of the history and plight of many Native Canadians as well as some misconceptions concerning the Crawford case. That these victims were not part of mainstream society and that they inhabited an isolated underworld are precisely why we have to ask ourselves what role racism played in this tragedy. As for no one showing any concern for these women when they were alive, that was not the case. Shelley Napope's anxious parents, perplexed that their young daughter had simply vanished, had been in frequent contact with police. Eva Taysup's family had contacted police in Saskatoon, Kelvington, and Yorkton to file missing person reports, complete with recent photographs of Eva. And Steve Morningchild, Calinda Waterhen's father, went repeatedly to the police with concerns about his missing daughter. He was told that Calinda was alive and living somewhere in Saskatchewan. But it should come as no surprise if some of the victims' families felt uncomfortable turning to the police for help.

Beyond their immediate families and a few close friends, no one could have known that Shelley Napope, Calinda Waterhen, and Eva Taysup were missing. Is it not the duty of the police to inform the public when a family expresses concern that one of its members has unexpectedly dropped out of sight? A senior officer with the Saskatoon Police Service offers the explanation that hundreds of missing person reports are filed every year, making it impossible to publicize them all, and that many of these "missing persons" are runaways who return in a few days or are simply people who do not want to be found. That is cold comfort to families who have valid reasons for fearing that something has happened to a loved one.

The police officer also suggests that the responsibility of

informing the media that someone is missing falls to the family. Obviously, only those with a certain sophistication, social status, and adequate resources are able to gain the ear of the media. Police procedure, in this case, may have served to further marginalize the Native families involved.

In his column, MacPherson correctly pointed out that if the trial had been in Toronto, it would have been national news. But as to the lack of compelling drama, one wonders what MacPherson considers compelling. There was an abundance of sex. There was murder and mutilation. There was a depraved, slack-jawed predator supported at every turn by his devoted mother. There was an unscrupulous informer who earned more than $15,000 for his efforts to trap Crawford and, in the process, avoided being named as a co-accused in at least one of the murders at which he had been present. Finally, there was a world-renowned forensic anthropologist who, with a handful of bones and a dearth of evidence, eventually brought a serial killer to trial.

It sounds like a fairly compelling drama by any standards.

And yet, most members of the general public don't even recognize the name of John Martin Crawford. He's no Clifford Olson. Certainly he's no Paul Bernardo. In his home town of Saskatoon, he doesn't even rank with the likes of David Threinen, the man who killed four Saskatoon youngsters in a murderous rampage twenty-five years ago.

Crawford's comfortable obscurity may not be a bad thing. The tragedy is that we don't remember Mary Jane Serloin, Shelley Napope, Eva Taysup, or Calinda Waterhen, either.

Perhaps we can begin to redress the balance.

Chapter One

"I Thought Her Name Was Angie . . ."

"John, for Christ's sake, what did you do?"
—Bill Corrigan

In the spring of 1992 Bill Corrigan was in his early forties. He was a diminutive character with a slight pot-belly and an extensive criminal record, mostly for minor offences such as fraud and passing bad cheques. He wore cowboy boots to boost his stature, and he was rarely without his buck knife with its gold handle and Oriental decorations. He craved respect, but on the street he was known as a man who could neither hold his liquor nor back up his bravado with his fists.

He did have a few violent crimes to his credit, including armed robbery. It was this latter transgression, the most serious of his career, that earned him a ten-year sentence in the federal corrections system. Armed with a rifle, he had attempted to rob a store in Brandon, Manitoba, his home town. Like most things in his life, it went wrong, and he eventually wound up in the

Saskatchewan Penitentiary in Prince Albert, where he shared accommodation with some of the country's most notorious felons.

It was in Prince Albert that Corrigan met John Martin Crawford. Housed in a unit with thirteen other inmates, Crawford and Corrigan became friends, insofar as either of them was capable of friendship. What it amounted to was trading lurid stories and making plans for the day they would be paroled. For Crawford, who was also serving a ten-year sentence, that day came in September 1987 when he was granted day parole and released into the custody of his mother, Victoria Crawford, who operated a group home for indigent men in Saskatoon. Within five months he was back inside and didn't see the light of day again until March 1989, when he was at the two-thirds point of his original sentence and automatically eligible for the same type of parole. Bill Corrigan, on his release in 1991, was anxious to be reunited with the companion of his confinement; to Corrigan, Crawford was a man who offered the promise of adventure. Consequently, Corrigan made Saskatoon his new home. He spent thirty days in the Salvation Army Hostel for men before moving down the street to the Albany Hotel.

The Albany is a neighbourhood pub where old friends gather for a beer and to share jokes with the barmaids, many of whom have been working there for years. It is also the watering hole of choice for much of the city's criminal element. It faces the Barry Hotel across 20th Street West in the heart of what passes for skid row in Saskatoon. Both hostelries have seen their share of stabbings and shootings. In 1990 Jake Badger, a popular bouncer, had been stabbed to death in the beverage room of the Albany by the brother and sister team of David and Margaret McDonald. In 1992 a healthy underground economy continued to thrive. Clothes, jewellery, and food liberated from stores in the nearby mall were continually on offer in the beverage room, and pimps and drug dealers went about their business virtually unimpeded. It was the kind of place to which Bill Corrigan would naturally and habitually gravitate. He moved into Room 2, and soon talked his way into occasional work such as cleaning, unloading the beer trucks, and other odd jobs.

Thirty-year-old John Crawford was a regular visitor. Arriving in his mother's early 1970s-vintage, green Chevy Nova, he would check at the registration desk to see if Corrigan was in. He almost always was. Despite the macho image he tried to present to the world, the older man rarely strayed from the security of his hotel room. Crawford would give Corrigan enough money to buy a case of beer, then the pair would be ready for their version of a good time.

The pattern rarely varied. They cruised the streets, looking for women. Crawford knew many of the hookers who worked the area, which included the strip on 20th Street and the quieter seven or eight blocks of 21st Street that had become known as the city's official "stroll." But Crawford was known as a bad trick. He abused the girls and did not like to pay the going rate. Even so, there was usually someone willing to go with him: a newcomer who hadn't heard of him, or a girl so drunk or stoned she was unable to resist him. There were others, too: young women who were not professionals in the sex industry but were willing to go for a ride if the offer included alcohol or drugs.

Shelley Napope was such a girl. Born into the One Arrow First Nation, she had been living in the city for almost eight of her sixteen years. Her parents had moved to Saskatoon after their house on the reserve, located eighty kilometres north of the city, was vandalized and demolished.

Shelley was a pretty girl, and popular among the 20th Street crowd. At sixteen she had developed a network of friends that supplied her with drugs and booze. As a consequence, she also had a record as a young offender. Outgoing and gregarious, she regularly made the rounds of the bars, but rarely stopped in any one place for long. On one of these flying visits early in 1992, she had met John Martin Crawford. When she ran into him again one evening that summer, she stopped for a chat. He was with Bill Corrigan in his mother's car in the parking lot behind the Albany Hotel.

Crawford recognized her immediately, and asked what she was up to. Shelley replied, "Not much," and asked the two men for a ride to Confederation Park, a west-side neighbourhood of modest '70s-style family homes and duplexes. "I've got to see some people out there," she said.

"No problem," Crawford responded. "Jump in."

Corrigan, according to routine, got in the back seat. Shelley sat in the front beside Crawford. When the trio arrived at Shelley's destination, the girl ran into the house while the men waited in the car. Crawford drummed his fingers impatiently on the steering wheel as he waited for her to return. He had earlier injected himself with methylphenidate hydrochloride, commonly known as Ritalin, a drug prescribed largely by psychiatrists for the treatment of Attention Deficit and Hyperactivity Disorder, or ADHD, mostly in children and adolescents. Through the same reckless experimentation that someone years ago had discovered that Talwin, an oral painkiller, provides an incredible "octane boost" when you dissolve a tablet in water and inject it into your arm, Ritalin was gaining popularity on the street as the intravenous drug of choice for many users. Crawford was feeling its effects, and was eager to begin the evening's activities.

Five minutes later a smiling Shelley Napope emerged from the house and got back into the car.

"What took you so long?" Crawford demanded. "I haven't got all night!"

In this, at least, he was telling the truth: his mother wanted the car back by nine o'clock. If it wasn't, Crawford would lose the privilege of using it for a few days.

"You guys got some beer?" Shelley asked.

"Sure," Corrigan piped up from the back seat. "You going to help us drink it?"

Crawford drove east out of Confederation Park, as if he were taking Shelley back downtown. She showed neither surprise nor concern when, instead, he turned onto Avenue H and headed south. She did not know, and Corrigan had apparently forgotten, that Crawford had borrowed Corrigan's knife earlier at the Albany and had not returned it.

The route took them down to Spadina Crescent West, past the Queen Elizabeth Power Station and onto a gravel road that followed the banks of the South Saskatchewan River out of the city. Within a few minutes they turned left onto Valley Road, a paved stretch of rural highway that was rapidly developing into a prosperous commercial district, featuring garden centres, berry farms, and, further along, the recently developed Moon Lake Golf and Country Club. Crawford knew the road well.

As Shelley fiddled with the radio, he flirted with her, stroking her leg and brushing his hand against her breast. Again, if she was nervous, she didn't show it. *These two are obviously losers*, she might have thought. *How dangerous can they be?* She had been in situations like this before and nothing horrible had happened. Well, not quite. Once a white man had raped her in his shack on Avenue M South, but she wouldn't be that stupid again. Besides, she had met Crawford before. He was overweight and he smelled like sweat and chemicals, but he didn't really seem that bad. She would drink his beer and party a little, then they would take her back downtown.

Twenty minutes after leaving the city, Crawford turned onto a dirt road. The battered Nova bounced and shuddered in the washboard ruts. To one side was a tree farm, to the other a farmer's field. The road led to Bare Ass Beach, a popular summer destination for uninhibited Saskatonians who found the expanse of river sand an ideal place to doff their clothes and soak up some sun. But it was evening, and there was no other traffic.

Before the turnoff to the beach, Crawford coaxed the Nova off the road and drove as carefully as his diminishing patience would allow across a stubble field to a grove of trees. Crawford knew the place well, but perhaps Shelley was surprised to find a natural clearing defined by willows. There was ample evidence of earlier parties—soggy beer boxes, empty cans and bottles, a blackened pit where fires had burned that summer—but tonight the grove was deathly still. Perhaps, too, she was surprised at the ribbons she saw hanging from trees, the tobacco pouches, and the piles of willow branches that had been used for sweat lodges that had subsequently been dismantled on instructions from an Elder. The grove was well known to First Nations people as well, not as a party venue but as a site for traditional ceremonies.

Or perhaps, in the last few minutes of her life, she noticed none of these things.

Crawford drove through a cut in the grove and parked the car out of sight. He turned off the engine and tossed the keys to Corrigan in the back seat. He ordered his friend to get the beer. Obediently, the little man got out and opened the trunk, removing the case of Pilsner he had purchased with Crawford's money earlier that evening. Back in the car, he handed Crawford a bottle. He opened another and passed it to Shelley. The two men gossiped about mutual acquaintances they had known in jail while Shelley made short work of her beer. She was after a quick buzz, nothing more. Corrigan and Crawford were not exactly stimulating companions.

Noticing Shelley's empty bottle, Crawford told Corrigan to go for a walk. Corrigan had played the scene enough by now to know his role by heart. "Don't do anything I wouldn't do," he said, laughing at the tired old joke as he closed the car door behind him. Beer in hand, he strolled a few metres away, then stopped to roll a cigarette.

Back in the car, Crawford was making his pitch: he wanted sex, and he wasn't about to pay for it. After all, he had supplied the beer and given her a ride to her friends' place. If Shelley wasn't game, she would suffer the consequences.

Shelley wasn't game, but she knew she didn't have many options. She was probably frightened by now. But the beer was working, and that might help. She could only hope that this rank thirty-year-old would be quick. If she closed her eyes, it would be over in a few minutes. They climbed into the back seat.

While Crawford abused her body, perhaps Shelley allowed herself to travel back to One Arrow, where she remembered real friends and community. Or perhaps she thought of a better life, the one she would have when she left the street and went back to school. She wanted to take a computer course. She knew she was better than this. She didn't belong in this world of round-the-clock partying, drugs, and flophouses. But she was only sixteen. There was lots of time to get her life together.

Crawford's act did not take long, and Corrigan soon heard

him shouting at Shelley in the car. "You bitch! You know you liked it! Don't look so pissed off!"

But Shelley too obviously had not enjoyed it, and John Crawford was enraged. He slapped the young woman across the side of the head. Shelley screamed and grabbed for the door handle, trying to get out. Crawford pulled her back and punched her full in the mouth, splitting her lip.

Outside, shivering in the cool evening air, Corrigan watched as Crawford stumbled out of the little Nova. The younger man opened a beer, breathing heavily as he began to drink. Corrigan said nothing, but watched again as Crawford threw open the rear door of the car. He saw that Shelley was naked and crying, and her face was battered.

"Tell him to take me home," she pleaded. "I just want to go back to the city. I won't go to the cops."

Corrigan had no time to consider her appeal, as Crawford reached in and started pulling Shelley out of the car by one arm.

"I'm not done with you yet," he declared. "We're going into those bushes and you're going to give me what I want!"

Dragging the nude and now-hysterical young woman from the car, Crawford hit her a few more times, then she fell to the ground. Corrigan got into the car to warm up as Crawford dragged the screaming girl into the bushes.

"It looked like he was punching her in the stomach," he testified later in court.

When Shelley fell silent, Corrigan became curious. He got out of the car and went to investigate. Crawford was standing over Shelley. A knife—Corrigan's own precious knife with the gold handle—was protruding from her abdomen. There were other wounds, too, Corrigan saw. Shelley had been stabbed repeatedly in the chest and side.

Dumbfounded, he said, "John, for Christ's sake, what did you do?"

"I killed her," Crawford replied without emotion or apparent regret. "She's dead. Get some branches. Help me cover her up."

Corrigan gathered branches and leaves and spread them carefully over the body, keeping a careful eye on Crawford as he did so.

The murderer had removed the knife from Shelley's abdomen and was holding it as he watched Corrigan do his bidding. Once the body was covered, the two men drove back to Saskatoon. Corrigan, animated and frightened, castigated Crawford for the senseless killing; at the same time, he harboured justifiable fears for his own life, so he was careful not to go too far in his condemnation.

Crawford pulled into an alley in Riversdale, a lower-income neighbourhood that hugs the west bank of the Saskatchewan River south of downtown. He rolled Shelley's clothes into a ball and tossed them in a dumpster. He had already decided to burn his own clothes and throw the knife into the river under the Broadway Bridge. He planned to return to the grove and knock out Shelley's teeth, so that the corpse, if it was ever found, could not be identified through dental records, though he never carried out this plan.

In the meantime, his curfew was approaching. With Corrigan still in the car, he drove home to his mother's house on Avenue Q North. There he removed his bloodstained jeans and sweatshirt, and showered in the basement bathroom. He then drove Corrigan back to the Albany.

By the time the remains of Shelley Napope were found in the fall of 1994, there was little physical evidence left to aid investigators in determining what had taken place on the night she was killed. Given the degree of decomposition of the body, it was impossible even to establish a probable cause of death. The only people who knew what had happened were John Crawford and Bill Corrigan.

That both men were present at the rape and murder of the young Native woman was never an issue. Crawford and Corrigan both agreed, subsequently, on the circumstances that led to her being taken to the willow grove southwest of Saskatoon. On audio tapes secretly recorded by the RCMP, Crawford—in calm, clipped tones, as if he were discussing the weather—clearly confirms many of the specifics of Shelley's murder. His only surprise was her name.

"I thought her name was Angie," he said.

Chapter Two

THE DISCOVERY

If there were more bodies in this eerie place, investigators might have a serial killer on their hands.

It was one of those splendid, warm autumn days that Saskatchewan people embrace with thankfulness and a hint of foreboding.

By October 1, most farmers have their crop in the bin and are going about the fall chores, knowing the inevitable five or six months of prairie winter are just around the corner. Urban folks are closing up the cabin at their lakeside properties and preparing their city homes for the onslaught of winter.

For Brian Reichert, an employee at the AgPro Grain terminal in Saskatoon, the pleasant weekend in October 1994 provided an ideal opportunity to spend a few hours tramping through the bush near the South Saskatchewan River southwest of Saskatoon. He wasn't much of a hunter, but when a friend had suggested they do a little spotting for deer on Saturday morning, he couldn't resist. The morning air was warm, the sun was strong, and the two men were anxious to get some fresh air and exercise. If they actually saw any deer, white-tails or mules, that would be a bonus.

The land was owned by Bill Hnatiuk, who ran a farm in the southern tip of the sprawling Rural Municipality of Corman Park, a generally prosperous blend of agricultural ventures and country residential developments surrounding Saskatoon. Around noon, after wandering through dense bush for more than two hours, Reichert happened upon a startling sight. He moved a little closer and reached down to pick up what was clearly a human skull. Nearby, he saw a few smaller bones and a patch of dark hair. Intrigued, he and his friend did some poking around. They didn't discover any more bones, but as their search widened they realized they had come across the remnants of an aboriginal spiritual ceremony. About fifty metres from where they found the skull, they saw colourful ribbons hanging from trees. Some of them were wound around open tobacco pouches. The four colours of the *wapanesenam*, or blessed cloth, represent the cardinal directions, and are presented along with tobacco to an Elder by someone seeking a favour. Cans of fruit had been placed at the base of a tree from which the banners were hung.

The discovery of the skull perplexed and unsettled Reichert, but he was not keen to get involved in a police matter. His companion, who remained anonymous throughout the investigation, wanted nothing to do with the police or anyone else who might ask probing questions. According to Reichert, the man was something of a recluse: "He's a good person and we're good friends, but he's kind of in a world of his own."

Reichert suffered from witness anxiety for the rest of the day, then finally decided that he had to report his findings to the police. That night he called the RCMP detachment on 8th Street in Saskatoon.

Constable Terry Stirling, a twenty-seven-year veteran of the force, met Reichert at the turnoff to the Moon Lake Golf and Country Club early the following morning. With Reichert giving directions, the two men drove the three kilometres or so to the grove across the road from Bare Ass Beach. Reichert led the officer into the bushes. A couple of minutes later, Stirling was staring at a human skull and other bones that he recognized as hips, ribs, and larger arm or leg bones. He photographed the site and performed a cursory search of the area before returning to the city, where he hoped to contact Dr. Ernie Walker.

Walker, a professor of anthropology at the University of Saskatchewan, is a man of extraordinary expertise in the fields of biological anthropology and forensic anthropology. For over twenty-five years he has been assisting police departments in Canada and the United States when unexplained bones turn up. He has identified hundreds of skeletal remains for police forces in numerous jurisdictions. He has worked with conservation officers, identifying bones they have come across as human or animal. He has testified for the prosecution in more than two dozen cases, and has spearheaded numerous investigations in which skeletal remains were all the police had to go on. Widely published in professional books and journals, he has a particular interest in Central Plains aboriginal cultures, and several of his articles have dealt with the analysis of burial sites. The RCMP recognized his contributions to investigations by appointing him a Supernumerary Special Constable in August 2000.

Walker was born and raised in west-side Saskatoon, where he attended King George Elementary School and Bedford Road Collegiate before studying at the University of Saskatchewan. It was at the University of Texas, where he earned his Ph.D., that he got his first taste of forensic anthropology. By the time he returned to Canada in 1981, he was already in demand by law enforcement agencies, particularly the RCMP in Saskatchewan.

"I'm very good at what I do," he explains matter-of-factly, and his work is a reflection of that knowledge. A fit fifty-one-year-old with piercing blue eyes that appear constantly to be searching for information, Walker eschews the image of the expert for hire who provides testimony on demand, collects an enormous fee, then goes chasing the next ambulance. In fact, he refuses to charge for his services to the RCMP. "It's not that I don't value what I do," he says, "but this is the way it should be." The university allows him time off to do forensic work, in the certainty that he brings as much back to the institution as he gives. For more than twenty years, Walker's profile and reputation have been a source of pride both to his department and to the university at large.

Clearly, Walker was the right man for the task of determining what they were dealing with at the Moon Lake site. Unfortunately, he was not available to go out to the site until Tuesday, October 4, three days after Reichert's discovery. Upon viewing the remains, though, the professor knew immediately that this was no archaeological find. There was considerable soft tissue present, and a matte of hair; neither would be found in archaeological material. This was a legal case, or at least a medical one. His preliminary examination told him that the victim was a woman, likely in her early twenties.

RCMP investigators gathered all the physical evidence they could find on the site, photographing and videotaping the scene at both ground level and from the air. Then they moved on to the second phase of the mystery: identifying the woman. While Ernie Walker worked on the remains in the morgue at Royal University Hospital, determining the victim's race, age, height, and time of death, the team of RCMP investigators began talking to sources, poring over intelligence reports, and preparing dental records that would be sent to local dentists for comparison. Sergeant Colin Crocker of the General Investigation Section (GIS) at the Saskatoon detachment headed the team. The identification officer was Constable Wayne Wiebe, who had before him a gargantuan task in terms of gathering and cataloguing evidence.

Media coverage got off to an inauspicious start in the Saskatoon *StarPhoenix*, the city's only daily newspaper. A brief story under the headline "Human remains unearthed" appeared on October 7; almost a week after Reichert had found the bones and three days after the RCMP had become involved. The story incorrectly stated that RCMP officers and Ernie Walker had been taken to the scene on Tuesday by "the hunter who found her." It also flubbed the location: Spadina Crescent, the street named in the story, ends within the city limits, several kilometres from the grove where the remains were actually found. The story did, however, begin to reveal the skills of Dr. Walker, who had quickly established from the skeleton alone that the victim was a female about twenty years of age.

A week later, on October 13, the RCMP had a second mystery on its hands. An elderly man out for his morning walk along a gravel road fifteen kilometres west of Saskatoon thought he spotted a deer lying in a clump of trees on the east side of the road. Coming closer, he gaped with horror at the sight of a young woman, nude, with a plastic bag over her head. She was Janet Sylvestre, a thirty-seven-year-old mother of two, originally from La Loche, Saskatchewan.

The following day RCMP Corporal Jerry Wilde, media relations officer for the Saskatoon detachment, led a gaggle of reporters out to the scene west of the city. But by the time the media arrived, there was little to see. Janet Sylvestre's body had been removed, and the area had been searched. While television photographers strained to find something to shoot, reporters wondered aloud why Wilde had invited them to an impromptu news conference beside a country road on a rainy Friday morning.

Meanwhile, the Moon Lake site was still under investigation. On October 21, Corporal Robert Todd drove out to the grove. Todd was a recent addition to the Saskatoon detachment, having arrived for duty with the GIS on September 1. He was accompanied by Staff Sergeant Bob Stair, an RCMP officer from Regina. Now retired from the force, Stair had spent much of his RCMP career with the Identification Unit, and had developed a particular expertise in crime scenes. When he learned that skeletal remains had been found near Saskatoon, his interest was piqued. But it was Bob Todd who made the discovery.

As he tells it, he was just wandering through the bush, with no clear plan in mind. He was thirty or forty metres west of where the first set of remains had been found when he looked back and saw "something white" protruding from the ground. On closer examination, he realized it was a human skull. Sergeant Stair immediately confirmed it. Wayne Wiebe, the identification officer, was called to the site as Todd strung yellow police tape around the fresh crime scene.

With two sets of unidentified remains within fifty metres of one another, the RCMP began to suspect that it had happened upon a dumping ground. Other information the officers had garnered but were not yet sharing with the public tended to confirm this conjecture. If there were more bodies in this eerie place, investigators might have a serial killer on their hands. A trained search team was brought in. Officers were positioned three metres apart and fanned out to search the area on a systematic grid.

Constable John Hudak found the next bone. It was poking through the ground within a foot of where he was standing. Next to it was the hollow orbit of a human skull just visible on the surface.

By the end of October 1994, it was official: four people were dead, including Janet Sylvestre, the only victim whose identity was known. The search for the person or persons who had committed the murders and callously discarded their bodies to decompose on the prairie was under way.

In reality, there were three investigations. The first, carried out largely by Ernie Walker, was directed at discovering the identities of the three young women whose bodies had been reduced to bones near Moon Lake. The other two investigations were carried out by the team headed by Sergeant Crocker, a twenty-five-year veteran of the force. For Crocker, who had been transferred to Saskatoon on October 1 and began his duties on the 11th, it was a baptism of fire. Whereas the work of the forensic anthropologist was followed closely by local media who were intrigued by the challenge of giving names to anonymous bones, Crocker's hunt for the killer or killers was carried out behind a shroud of silence and half-truths, for reasons known only to the police.

In true Mountie tradition, the force was going to get its man. But it was not about to let anyone know that it already had a suspect in its sights. The genuine investigation, then, was aimed at building a case against John Martin Crawford without John Martin Crawford—or anyone else, for that matter—finding out. The third investigation was not really an investigation at all.

It was a construction of smoke and mirrors that the media and the people of Saskatoon were permitted to hear about and occasionally participate in. It was a puzzling and unusual tactic, with little justification and less value. Nonetheless, the RCMP defends it, although at least one member of the investigation team conceded it was unlike anything he had encountered in his fifteen-year tenure with the force.

Beginning at the grove and then in the morgue, Ernie Walker set out to recover all traces of bone and other material that remained at the site. At the scene of the first discovery, crawling on their hands and knees through thick bush, he and other searchers were able to find more than 90 percent of the skeleton, although it was widely dispersed over a 520-square-metre area. The larger bones showed signs of carnivore chewing, while the smaller bones of the hands and feet had evidently been consumed. Whoever killed the woman had made no attempt to bury the body, and coyotes and roving farm dogs had obviously found the remains. Considering what he had to work with, Walker knew he would be unable to pinpoint the cause of death. In his notes, though, he observed that the victim had practised good dental hygiene—a fact that would, ironically, impede the process of identification. He was further able to determine that she was between sixteen and twenty-three years of age, was approximately 165 centimetres (5′5″) tall, and probably Native, although he refused to confirm that at this point.

At the second Moon Lake site, Walker was able to gather human remains within a twenty-five-square-metre area, ultimately accounting for some 85 percent of the skeletal system. Unlike the first victim, this woman had poorly aligned teeth. This would greatly assist in identifying her once composite sketches were prepared. Walker was certain she was Native, likely in her mid to late teens.

From skulls alone, Walker is able to determine the sex, racial origin, and approximate age of the victim. He looks first for twelve anatomical features, which he records as male or female. The size of the mastoid process behind the ear, for example, is generally larger in males than in females. Walker was able to identify ten female characteristics on the first skull found. But the bones of the pelvis and hips are also important in determining sex, wider hips being indicative of a female. The degree of fusion of specific bones, particularly in the pubic region, is a good indicator of age, while the shape of the jaw and nose, as well as the distance between the eyes, help in determining racial affiliation.

The third site was a different matter, for the victim had been buried in a shallow grave. The murderer's attempt to conceal his crime had been so half-hearted, however, that it only added to the horror of the scene. The skull, whitened from exposure, protruded just above the ground. The distal humerus, a portion of the upper arm, was also poking through the soil, the hand and forearm missing. The crime scene promised to provide investigators with considerably more physical evidence than had the first two. But it was late October. The days were getting shorter and the weather steadily more miserable as Walker and his RCMP colleagues laboured to conduct a scientific excavation of the remains. Carefully removing dirt, leaves, and other foreign material, the team dug beneath the body and inserted a sheet of plywood. The corpse had been wrapped in a blanket and tied with an orange extension cord. It emerged from the ground relatively undisturbed, and was immediately taken to the morgue at Royal University Hospital for a post-mortem examination. Inside the gruesome package, Walker found the body of a young woman, lying on her stomach. Her head was turned to the right, her legs crossed. Walker knew she would divulge many more secrets than the bones of her sisters had provided.

When there is soft tissue remaining, there will also be insects. With a disciplined mind and a strong stomach, the forensic investigator with a knowledge of the larval growth and life cycles of creatures such as the cottonwood histor beetle, a common species in the Saskatchewan parklands, can pinpoint the time of death with remarkable accuracy. Of greater significance in this case was the presence of flies, specifically the Regina species, more commonly known as the black blowfly. These creatures feed on the tissues and lay their eggs in the bodies of decomposing animals— or in this case, a human being. The structure of the pupa casings told Walker a great deal about the time of death, suggesting that the woman had been killed in the spring, since the black blowfly breeds in cooler weather and is the first fly to lay its eggs. Since there was no evidence of bottle flies, which breed in warmer weather, Walker was even more confident that the woman had died in the spring, most likely within two or three years of the body being found.

Walker then turned his attention to the woman's physical characteristics. He estimated her to be twenty-nine to thirty-two years of age, 160 to 170 centimetres (5'3"–5'7") tall, and with a stocky build. Her left arm had not been cut off by any natural occurrence, such as the chewing of dogs or other animals. It had clearly been sawed through above the elbow, while the arm was fully extended. The lower portion of the arm had been removed after death. Her jaw had been broken around the time of death, as well as at least one rib on her left side. Her nose had been broken years earlier.

The shovel-shaped teeth told Walker that the victim was a First Nations person. Brown stains indicated that she had been a smoker, and there was clear evidence of periodontal disease. The teeth would later be x-rayed and examined by Dr. Sandy Myers, a forensic odontologist at the University of Saskatchewan, and would prove extremely helpful in identifying this woman who had suffered a horrible death in 1991 or 1992.

Less than a week after the first remains had been found at the Moon Lake site, the name of John Martin Crawford cropped up in the GIS office in Saskatoon. It had been known in the Customs and Excise Section for some time before that.

Stan Lintick, a corporal with Customs and Excise since 1989, had been using Bill Corrigan as a paid informant since 1993. Corrigan had first approached the Mounties with information about illegal cigarette sales at the Can Tho restaurant on 20th Street, half a block from the Albany Hotel. Lintick assigned the informant a registration number, and Corrigan soon earned a measure of credibility with his RCMP handlers. His information generally proved accurate, and resulted in convictions. He picked up a few hundred dollars for his efforts, as well as a reputation for reliability in the circumscribed subculture of stool pigeons and rats.

So when Corrigan called Stan Lintick in July 1993 with information about an alleged homicide, he was taken seriously. Lintick was on holiday, so it was Constable Malcolm Eskelson, a member of the Federal Enforcement Unit, who took the call. Corrigan's story lacked detail, and didn't ring true; nonetheless, Eskelson arranged to meet him near the Albany Hotel. Fifteen minutes later the informant was in the police car, nervously relating a story that Eskelson knew from long experience fell considerably short of the whole truth.

Corrigan knew something about the killing of a girl named Angie, he said. Two men named John Crawford and John Potter were involved. He offered to show Eskelson where the murder had been committed, and subsequently directed him to an area south of Saskatoon. He pointed out a turnoff into a grove of trees. Eskelson drove through the bush and turned the car around in a hay field while Corrigan expanded on his story. Neither man got out of the car. Indeed, they were soon heading back to Saskatoon. Before they reached the city, however, Corrigan had admitted that he and John Crawford, in an apparently separate but related incident, had once picked up a girl named Angie, who was about seventeen years old, and driven her out to an area near Bare Ass Beach. Crawford had dropped Corrigan off on the riverbank with a six-pack of beer, he claimed, and then picked him up afterwards and they drove back to the city. Oddly, Corrigan could not remember if Angie had returned to the city with them. The tale was vague, at best, and the parts about the mysterious John Potter, whom Corrigan claimed had moved to the West Coast, were puzzling; and doubly puzzling when efforts to locate Potter through the usual methods—police computers, social services, phone books—came up empty.

Lintick returned from holidays in the first week of August, and Eskelson told his colleague of the bizarre encounter he had had with the equally peculiar Bill Corrigan. Lintick took it under advisement. In cases of suspected homicide, officers in the Customs and Excise Section would normally write an intelligence report and turn it over to the General Investigation Section. Lintick had developed a good working relationship with Corrigan, and though he filed his report, he wasn't yet ready to step aside.

He contacted his informant. As might have been expected, Corrigan went on at length about the mythical John Potter, the man who could fill in the blanks for the Mounties. He also regaled the corporal with tales of women's clothing that he had seen in the trunk of John Martin Crawford's car. Lintick was deeply suspicious of his informant's ramblings, but when Corrigan volunteered the comment that "there's one body out there if there's not more," he knew he had to take action. Buoyed by the knowledge that Corrigan had been useful in the past, Lintick arranged for a search dog to be brought down from Prince Albert.

On August 5, Lintick, the dog, and its master went to the spot Corrigan had pointed out in the grove south of the city. While Lintick waited on the road, the dog and its master roamed through the area. The whole search took just a few minutes. The dog found no evidence of a body. As Lintick later said, "You could've walked over those bones ten times and never see them" because of the tall grass and the undergrowth. Why the dog didn't smell them is anybody's guess.

Lintick was not content to leave it at that. In the weeks that followed, when he wasn't chasing moonshiners or pursuing cigarette and liquor smugglers through the landscape and the courts, Lintick allowed himself to ponder the story Bill Corrigan had told him. More than once he drove out to the grove with his informant, and sometimes he went on his own. Walking in the deep grass between the overhanging willows, or just sitting in his car surveying the scene with questioning eyes, he would ask himself again and again if there was any substance in Corrigan's unlikely tale.

Lintick had his answer when the bones of a murdered woman turned up in the grove he had been visiting off and on for fourteen months. The search dog, he realized when he visited the scene, had been no more than ten or fifteen metres from the skeletal remains Brian Reichert found on October 1, 1994.

Although Lintick was assigned to Customs and Excise, he spent much of the following month working on the murder investigation. He had not seen Bill Corrigan since February. The first task, then, was to find him. It wasn't difficult. Corrigan, never a man of high intelligence, had fled Saskatoon in 1994 after relieving his employers at the Albany Hotel of $1,680 he had been entrusted to place in a night deposit. Lintick traced him through Manitoba Social Services, and soon found him in Winnipeg, collecting welfare and working part time as a school crossing guard.

Sergeant Colin Crocker decided to send Lintick to Winnipeg with Constable Al Keller, who had been assigned to the case. Keller, in common with a remarkable number of officers of the GIS, was relatively new to the unit. He had arrived in Saskatoon in July 1994 after three years in nearby Delisle, a satellite operation responsible to the Saskatoon detachment. But though he may have come into the investigation with little experience in homicide cases, what he lacked in experience he made up for in enthusiasm and intelligence. Balding, bespectacled, short, and out of uniform, Keller looks more like an accountant than a cop. But he is a deceptively powerful man, and carries himself with confidence. As anyone who has run up against him will tell you, behind the warm smile and unassuming demeanour lurks a man with the tenacity of a pit bull. Before he was assigned to the Moon Lake investigation, his thirteen-year career included postings in Melville in southeastern Saskatchewan and Buffalo Narrows in the north, as well as Delisle, a town briefly famous in the 1970s as the location of the motion picture *Paperback Hero*, but more enduringly celebrated as the home town of the hockey-playing Bentley brothers.

Soon after joining the GIS, Keller was handed a thin file containing information about the alleged murder of a young woman named Angie in the Moon Lake, or Bare Ass Beach, area south of Saskatoon. The file, which contained Stan Lintick's report, had been opened in 1993. Keller knew the area well, as officers from both the Delisle and Saskatoon detachments as well as the Corman Park Municipal Police regularly patrol Bare Ass Beach and environs in the summer, on the lookout for young drinkers and other lawbreakers.

Keller inherited the file in mid-summer, when the willows and other vegetation are at their thickest and most lush near the river. He decided to postpone any more inspections of the grove until later in the season. In the meantime, he occupied himself with other matters, including the hunt for John Potter, whom Keller had pretty much decided did not exist. It was in mid-September that he arranged for another police dog to search the grove. But in two hours of sniffing and quartering and casting back and forth, this dog, too, failed to turn up anything useful.

The discovery of the bones on October 1 changed all that. By mid-October, Keller and Lintick were off to Winnipeg to pay a visit to Bill Corrigan.

Corrigan's face turned ashen as he looked through the peephole in the door of the apartment he shared with his girlfriend. Though dressed casually in blue jeans and jackets, the men on the other side of the door were easily recognizable as cops. The larger one, he knew, was Corporal Stan Lintick from Saskatoon. He didn't know the other.

The situation was not unfamiliar to Corrigan. He had been dealing with the police off and on for most of his life. What could they want this time? he wondered. Was it about the money he'd stolen from the Albany? No, they wouldn't come all the way to Winnipeg for that.

Had they found Angie?

He opened the door.

"Hi, Bill. How're you doing?" Lintick extended a large hand and grasped Corrigan's sweating palm. He introduced Constable Keller. "We'd like to talk to you about something."

"Sure, Stan." Corrigan was always eager to please. "What's it about?"

"It seems there was something in your story about Angie. We found some bones near Bare Ass Beach. We think it could be the girl you were talking about."

Corrigan didn't want his girlfriend listening. As it was Monday morning and he had to get to work, the three men grabbed a quick coffee in a nearby restaurant. As Corrigan chain-smoked and fidgeted, Keller studied his voice quirks and mannerisms. They made arrangements to meet later that day.

At four o'clock, the two Mounties collected Corrigan from his apartment and took him to their room in the Westin Hotel. Thus began several hours of intense questioning. Lintick, still technically with the Customs and Excise Section, listened and watched as his GIS colleague asked most of the questions. At first, Corrigan clung to his story about John Potter. The mythical Potter likely represented the only way Corrigan could see to get the gruesome story off his chest without implicating himself.

They paused for supper in the hotel, then returned to their room where the questioning continued. As the night wore on, Corrigan wore down. Keller and Lintick maintain they did nothing to intimidate their nervous informant, although terms such as "accessory after the fact" may have worked their way into the conversation. Using all the techniques he'd acquired through his training and experience, Keller began to gain Corrigan's trust. By ten o'clock, Corrigan agreed to make a recorded statement.

He talked for half an hour. One of the first things he disclosed was that John Potter did not exist. No one was really surprised by the admission, but Stan Lintick was heard to sigh deeply. He had spent hours, days even, trying to track down John Potter. Why couldn't the little weasel have come clean earlier? He did tell a compelling story, though. He gave details that only he or the killer could have known. Despite his history as a liar and a thief, he appeared to be speaking the truth on most points. He admitted that he had been along for the ride, but John Crawford was the murderer.

At the end of the evening, Keller was pleased with the progress they had made, but he was not satisfied that they had the whole story. The following day, he and Lintick took Corrigan to D Division headquarters in Winnipeg, where the informant gave two statements, one of which was videotaped. Corrigan's biggest worry, he admitted, was what John Crawford would do to him if he found out that he was talking to the police. That and the threat of prosecution stemming from the theft at the Albany made the prospects of returning to Saskatoon to testify distinctly unappealing. Corrigan was seriously spooked, but Keller was determined not to lose him. On returning to Saskatoon, he made it his business to speak to Corrigan on the phone several times a week, and arrangements were made so that Corrigan no longer had to worry about the Albany theft.

It was time to set the trap for John Martin Crawford.

Chapter Three

THE SNITCH

*"If all the evidence comes to fact, I would
hope we would be able to solve this. But right
now we're still grasping for straws."*

—Sergeant Colin Crocker
January 17, 1995

The remains of three unidentified women lay in a morgue. A
fourth woman, Janet Sylvestre, had been brutally murdered and
likely sexually assaulted. If there was any connection between
Janet's death and the three others, though, the RCMP wasn't
discussing it. With four homicides to contend with, Crocker's
GIS team could be forgiven if it was feeling a little over-
whelmed. And it had John Crawford to observe.

While Ernie Walker was completing his examination of the
unidentified remains in preparation for a comparison of dental
records and the creation of composite drawings, the media
speculated on whether the three bodies might be connected to

the so-called Hooker Wars that had made headlines in Saskatoon in the mid-1980s, and the RCMP quietly set up Special O, a surveillance squad whose sole purpose was to tail John Martin Crawford.

On October 11, 1994, five days after Sergeant Stan Lintick sat down with his colleagues to tell them what he knew about Bill Corrigan, John Martin Crawford, and the mythical John Potter, the surveillance team was in place. Corporal Robert Todd was assigned to co-ordinate it. An imposing figure, well over 190 centimetres (6′2″) tall and weighing nearly 113 kg (250 lb.) with long, dirty-blond hair that he often tied in a ponytail, the forty-something Todd appeared every inch the hard case he was supposed to portray under cover. As the co-ordinator of the team, Todd was not directly involved in the surveillance, but he spent hours listening on his police radio as the first-line officers kept tabs on their suspect. Cruising the red light district around Avenue P and 21st Street, Todd often passed Crawford wheeling his mother's newly purchased grey Mercury Cougar around the stroll. With Corrigan in Winnipeg, John had picked up a new travelling companion, a sinister-looking man named Jimmy Mason.* Todd once followed the pair into a Robin's Donuts at 22nd and Avenue P, where he bought a coffee and sat nearby, eavesdropping on their conversation and, more important, getting a good look at Crawford.

If the squad hoped to see firsthand evidence of Crawford's capacity for violence, they did not have long to wait. On the first night of the surveillance, Todd was giving his boss, the newly transferred Sergeant Colin Crocker, a tour of the primary target area and bringing him up to speed on the investigation. At about 8:30 PM, with two police constables observing from an unmarked car, John Crawford picked up a young woman (later identified as Theresa Kematch) on 21st Street, assaulted her, and dumped her in an out-of-the-way storage lot. By the time Todd and Crocker arrived on the scene, the inebriated but thoroughly terrorized victim was sitting on the curb, sobbing and holding

*Not his real name

her head. It was obvious that she had been beaten—her eyes and nose were swollen—and her pants were open, suggesting that there had been a sexual assault as well.

Taking charge of the situation, Todd asked her if she had been raped. The young woman denied it. She just wanted to go home, she said. Todd arrested her instead, and took her to the RCMP cells on 8th Street. She had nothing to say, to Todd or to anyone else. She was released the next morning and driven to her parents' home in Sutherland, an east-side neighbourhood that abuts the university farm.

Sergeant Crocker testified later that, given the victim's refusal to volunteer any information about the incident, it would have been next to impossible to lay a charge against Crawford. Yet the assault took place within three metres of two RCMP officers. At the very least, the police could have prevented the attack from happening in the first place. They chose not to.

After a long first night of surveillance, Special O was on the street again the following evening. Crocker, who had worked until two o'clock that morning, rode with Todd again. The rest of the team tailed Crawford as he trolled in circles around the stroll. But Crawford surprised the team by going home early. It was just before nine o'clock when he returned home—"home" being Victoria Crawford's large house at 113 Avenue Q North, a short two blocks from the hooker stroll her son loved to cruise. Crocker called an impromptu meeting of the surveillance team. Twenty minutes later he decided it was time to call it a night.

Fifteen blocks away, a woman known on the strip as Smiley was making the rounds of the downtown bars. She had a few drinks in the Barry, then, bored with the scenery, crossed the street to the Albany. She had lots of friends, as well as a few enemies, but finding someone to buy her a drink was rarely a problem. Several witnesses recalled seeing her in the bars that evening. At least one saw her leave with a large man around midnight. It was the last time Janet Sylvestre was seen alive.

When her body was found the next day, the RCMP had a new mystery as well as a bewildering set of side issues. It was possible that Crawford had slipped out of the house again after the surveillance team had withdrawn. It was equally possible, given the young man's history of violence in general and violence against Janet Sylvestre in particular, that Crawford had killed her in revenge for the ordeal she had put him through two years earlier. In 1992, after a violent episode in a house on Avenue Q, Janet had gone to the police and accused John Martin Crawford of rape. The charge had been stayed when Janet failed to show up for court, but John spent a month in jail before his mother put up $4,000 in bail.

As the investigation evolved, however, the RCMP became convinced that Crawford had not killed Sylvestre, despite having both motive and opportunity. The official line was that it was impossible to say if the witness at the bar had seen Smiley leaving with John Crawford. It might have been Jimmy Mason, or some other acquaintance. In the final analysis, the Mounties were unable to find any evidence tying the murder of Janet Sylvestre to the deaths of the three other women. Seven years later, they say they are no closer to finding Janet Sylvestre's killer.

Early on, investigators knew that Bill Corrigan was their best hope of building a case against John Martin Crawford. There was little in the way of physical evidence other than the blanket and the orange extension cord that had been buried with the third victim. Much as everybody might have wished it otherwise, Bill Corrigan was the one irreplaceable sprocket in the machine they had built to gather evidence against a murderer.

Corrigan was no pillar of the community. His handlers were justifiably fearful that the ex-con in his western shirts and pointed cowboy boots might just pick up and ride off into the metaphorical sunset. At the same time, they knew that eyewitnesses to murder are rarely motivated by abstract notions of virtue and good citizenship. If they have information, they usually want something for it. Bill Corrigan would have been the last person to break this mould. It was time to formalize a working arrangement with him.

Consequently, on October 22, 1994, Corrigan, accompanied by

Corporal Stan Lintick, was brought to Saskatoon for the day. Once on the ground, he was immediately taken to the grove near Bare Ass Beach where he had admitted to being with Crawford and the girl he still called Angie. As officers videotaped the scene, Corrigan described what had happened that spring night in 1992. Corrigan was paid $300 plus expenses for his trouble, then flown back to Winnipeg on a commercial flight that evening.

By this time, it was becoming obvious even to Bill Corrigan that there was money to be made by co-operating with the RCMP. Perhaps it even paid better than crime. There were certainly fewer risks, and such considerations were important to a man whose criminal record contained more than fifty convictions, an extraordinarily high percentage of which had landed him in jail. While snitching on cigarette smugglers might bring him an occasional beating, or more often simply the threat of a beating, it brought in much-needed cash, and it was guaranteed not to land him in jail. He'd certainly been impressed when the Mounties forked over $300 for a quick visit to Saskatoon.

Within days of his return to Winnipeg, Corrigan received a call from F Division headquarters in Regina. The Royal Canadian Mounted Police—the Mounties—are organized according to geography and function, so while there are deputy commissioners in charge of the Pacific Region, the North West Region, the Central Region, and the Atlantic Region, there are also deputy commissioners in charge of such things as Organized Crime, Strategic Direction, and Corporate Management and Comptrollership. Both Manitoba and Saskatchewan are under the authority of the North West Region, with D Division headquarters located in Winnipeg and F Division headquarters and training academy in Regina, with larger or smaller detachments located throughout their respective territories.

An officer named Randy Koroluk from F Division had an offer Bill couldn't refuse. Al Keller had briefed Koroluk on the Saskatoon investigation. Keller had worked with informants before, and had attended a seminar on the art of negotiating, but he didn't feel qualified to handle the Corrigan agreement. When Corporal Koroluk arrived in Winnipeg, he picked up the ex-con at his apartment and escorted him to D Division headquarters. The corporal told Corrigan that he had a contract, and over the next two hours he explained its terms. The Mounties were prepared to give Corrigan $15,000 plus expenses, and they would cover any loss of income he might suffer as a result of his efforts on their behalf. Corrigan, in return, would travel to Saskatoon whenever necessary to aid the investigation and testify at a preliminary hearing or a trial. The $15,000 would be paid in two instalments: the first in January 1995, the balance at the conclusion of John Martin Crawford's murder trial. Thus, if Corrigan got cold feet or experienced a change of heart, he would be doing himself out of what was, in his terms, a great deal of money.

The prospect of collecting $15,000 of government money from the police would have a definite appeal to any virtually unemployable man eking out a meagre existence on welfare. To Corrigan it was not only a financial windfall; it was also a guarantee that the RCMP would not attempt to tie him to the murders as an accessory or even as co-defendant. It must have been with a considerable sigh of relief, then, that on November 16, 1994, he signed a letter of acknowledgement. He was in the clear. More than that, he was no longer a mere informant, lurking in the shadows and collecting cash for information; he was an agent for the Royal Canadian Mounted Police.

With Bill Corrigan securely in place, the investigation continued throughout the fall. Lack of manpower prevented the RCMP from maintaining their surveillance of John Martin Crawford around the clock, as they wished, but, with the one possible and tragic exception of Janet Sylvestre, it likely made no difference. Crawford's habits rarely varied. During the day he helped his mother, Victoria, with chores around the house. At night he borrowed his mom's Cougar and cruised the streets looking for hookers. Occasionally, he ventured downtown to the seedier bars on 20th Street, but he rarely drank much now. His only desire was to meet a woman with whom he could have sex.

Crawford was leading a less exciting life these days, compared to the previous two years. In 1992, the year he is believed to have started his killing spree, he was before the courts on several occasions. He spent weeks in remand at the Saskatoon Correctional Centre and at various alcohol- and substance-abuse treatment centres around the province. Two women claimed that he assaulted them that same year and an attack on a young man earned Crawford another year behind bars. But though he managed to avoid police charges in the autumn of 1994, his pattern remained consistent: he would hunt for women and have sex. The only difference was that the police were now watching him.

The investigation remained largely out of range of the myopic gaze of the local media. The citizens of Saskatoon, therefore, had no true inkling of the nature or extent of the crimes that had been committed—indeed, were still being committed—in their city. They had shown little concern, in any case, when the remains first came to light. Most people were interested in knowing who the three victims were, but many had already decided that they were probably hookers, and almost certainly Native. That the RCMP was less than forthcoming with the media when it claimed to have no leads in the case and kept the true nature of the investigation—that it might have a serial killer in its sights—a secret would likely have provoked little protest.

Crown prosecutor Terry Hinz, who was brought into the investigation immediately after the bodies were discovered in October, explains the lack of public concern in terms of "threat assessment": most people living in Saskatoon did not perceive any threat to their own lives. While it is true that most violent crime in Saskatoon takes place in a relatively compact, twenty-block area, and the people living in the city's more affluent neighbourhoods are safely distanced from it, the prostitutes who daily expose themselves to the perils of the world's most dangerous profession had a right to know that a predator was stalking them. By the same token, those less affluent citizens who live in Riversdale or Pleasant Hill or King George had a right to know that young women were being taken from their neighbourhood streets and killed.

But the prostitutes expressed little fear. Many of them, too, had decided that the three unknown victims were hookers. Violence went with the territory. As for Janet Sylvestre, well, she wasn't really one of them. Bill Thibodeau, who works with Egadz Youth Centre (an inner-city facility that runs a variety of programs for workers in the sex trade, particularly the very young), observed no overt panic among the women with whom he maintained almost daily contact. Cruising the same streets as John Crawford, only handing out sandwiches and hot drinks instead of looking for cheap sex, Thibodeau ran into two young girls who asked, "Murders, what murders?" For the others, he observed, it didn't seem to be a deterrent. Perhaps if these women and people like Bill Thibodeau had been aware of the true nature of the crimes and the danger of selling sex on Saskatoon streets in 1994, they would have reacted differently.

Official updates coming out of the RCMP office were vague, and gave no suggestion that investigators were well advanced in their efforts to apprehend the killer. Then Kim Rossmo, a criminologist from Simon Fraser University, threw a spanner into the works. When Rossmo, an erstwhile Saskatoon resident, suggested in the *StarPhoenix* that police could in fact be hunting for a serial killer, media relations officer Jerry Wilde was quick to downplay the suggestion. "Our first priority is to identify these people," he said tersely.

But Rossmo was obviously on to something. Despite the lack of public knowledge, he identified several factors in the case that fit the profile of the serial killer. Serial killing, by definition, involves three or more killings by a single person, in separate incidents, with a cooling-off period between them. The fact that the three bodies were found in three distinct places rather than in a single grave indicated that the murders had occurred at different times, but that one person was responsible. It was typical of serial killers to use the same dumping ground time after time, Rossmo noted. They generally dispatch their victims and leave them where the deed was done. They rarely bury them or try to hide them.

"This guy's taking them here because it's a good hiding spot," he said, observing that serial killers often favour lovers' lanes or drinking spots used by teenagers. "It could well be an area he was familiar with. Maybe he used to park there when he was younger." Rossmo suggested, further, that the RCMP should be looking for a local person, as 75 percent of serial killers strike close to home.

The day after the criminologist's opinions were reported by the media, Sergeant Colin Crocker issued what amounted to a rebuttal in the *StarPhoenix*. That the skeletal remains were found near a popular party site, he said, could mean that three or more individuals were responsible for the killings, and that they could have occurred on three separate occasions. No one was seriously disputing the latter. It was more smoke and mirrors. Crocker knew all he needed to know about identifying a serial killer, but he managed to sidestep the issue in the media without openly contradicting Rossmo's conclusions. The sergeant's motivations were not entirely clear at this point. What is clear is that by late October the police believed their suspect was a multiple murderer, but chose to keep Saskatonians in the dark about it.

As the investigation moved into November, the RCMP enlisted the help of other agencies to sift through the public records for reports of missing Native women in western Canada. In the end, the search turned up nearly five hundred women, reported missing in the previous three years, who matched the general criteria of age and background of the Saskatoon victims. Officials later disputed that number, but the number itself was almost irrelevant. Whether it was one hundred or five hundred, it was clear that something like an epidemic was raging virtually unchecked in western Canada. Whether by accident or design, choice or foul play, the whereabouts of an enormous number of aboriginal women were officially unknown.

Of the approximately 470 missing women on Colin Crocker's list, more than half were quickly eliminated as potential victims. But Saskatoon investigators did manage to turn up a number of local names that seemed to fit the descriptions Dr. Ernie Walker had come up with. In mid-November, the RCMP released two composite sketches by Cyril Chan, a technician with the Alberta Medical Examiner's office. Working closely with Dr. Walker, Chan had produced credible likenesses of all three murdered women. The first showed a young woman with strong Native features and poorly aligned teeth. The second was of a woman in her twenties with long dark hair, good teeth, and a face that suggested Native features, but less obviously than the other. The third bore a striking resemblance to a photograph the RCMP later provided to the media, although the sketch itself was not released with the other two. It was no longer necessary; investigators had identified her as Eva Taysup, a mother of four from the Yellow Quill First Nation near Rose Valley in central Saskatchewan. Hers were the remains that had been found wrapped in a blanket tied with an orange electrical cord and buried a few inches under the soil. The blanket and electrical cord were "holdback" evidence for the time being. Although news of the first real break in the case did make it onto the front page of the Saskatoon *StarPhoenix*, the day's news was dominated by another story. Robert Latimer, a farmer from the Wilkie area, had just been convicted of second-degree murder in the "mercy killing" of his twelve-year-old daughter, Tracy. So, Eva Taysup's identification did not receive the media attention it warranted.

Ernie Walker and his Alberta colleagues conceded that the composite sketches executed by Cyril Chan were, at best, only 60 to 70 percent accurate. Nonetheless, within a day of their release a minor flood of telephone calls began pouring into the GIS office. Every hint and clue and statement had to be checked and followed up. Officers renewed their efforts on the street, talking to people who may have known women resembling the ones whose faces had appeared on television or in the newspaper.

Sergeant Crocker was generally available for media interviews throughout the investigation. Unlike many senior officers, Crocker did not routinely deflect questions to his media relations officer, Corporal Jerry Wilde. Crocker spoke regularly to the *StarPhoenix* and usually granted requests for interviews from television and radio reporters. On one occasion he conducted an extensive interview with a reporter from *The Globe & Mail*—one of the few times the investigation took on national significance. During one two-week stretch, when Wilde was out of town, Crocker handled all calls that otherwise would have gone through the media relations office. It was a role he became comfortable in, if only because it allowed him personal control over the information that was released into the public domain.

In hindsight, it is apparent that he was providing the media with the journalistic equivalent of table scraps. Dozens of stories appeared after the bodies were found, but few had any substance. None told the real story. Crocker mused about possible scenarios, expressed sympathy for the victims and their families, and promised that the Mounties would do everything in their power to apprehend the person or persons responsible for the murders. He was cordial and quotable, but never truly candid.

"It had to be done that way," he claimed later. "We couldn't give up our hand."

On December 14, 1994, one more piece of the puzzle fell into place: Shelley Napope was identified as another of the victims. A friend from the 20th Street area had come forward with the information that he had not seen the girl for some time, but he remembered her and was able to provide a name. Dental records confirmed the identity of Shelley, a teenager from the Duck Lake area. Her family had reported her missing almost two years earlier. She would have been sixteen when she died.

Terry Hinz has successfully prosecuted more murderers than any other Crown attorney in Saskatchewan over his twenty-year career. His role in the early stages of the investigation was to assist the Mounties with strategy. For the most part, his relationship with his law enforcement colleagues was a good one, based on mutual respect. But he is easy to misjudge; his bookish appearance conceals a will of iron. Early on in the investigation he "got into a pissing match," as he put it, with an RCMP profiler the local GIS had brought in from Ottawa. The profiler wanted to put a tap on John Crawford's telephone. Hinz said it wouldn't be worth the effort. Their target was monosyllabic at the best of times, and it was known that his mother didn't like him receiving phone calls at home. For legal and tactical reasons, Hinz wanted to use a body pack. At the end of the day, he got his way. He usually does.

Hinz had become an authority in Saskatchewan on the use of wiretaps. Working with his boss, Regional Crown Prosecutor Fred Dehm, he prepared an application that would be presented to Mr. Justice W. F. (Frank) Gerein of the Saskatchewan Court of Queen's Bench. The order, authorized under Section 185 of the Criminal Code of Canada, was signed by Mr. Justice Gerein on December 21, 1994. It gave investigators permission to record conversations between three people: John Martin Crawford, William James Corrigan, and Jimmy Mason. The conversations could be recorded in any place Corrigan called home, in the Mercury Cougar owned by John Crawford's mother, Victoria, in the Crawford home at 113 Avenue Q North, and in the house occupied by Jimmy Mason. The authorization also spelled out the type of equipment that could be used, including a body pack and microphones that could be placed in vehicles or motel rooms. Bill Corrigan had agreed to wear a recording device as he engaged John Crawford in conversation about his attacks on Saskatoon women.

Crocker's team was ready to set the trap, but they gave no hint of the true nature of the investigation to the media. On January 6, 1995, he beguiled a *StarPhoenix* reporter with rambling thoughts about the four murders, asking for information from the public, all the while maintaining he wasn't sure if the Sylvestre case fit into the larger puzzle.

"At times I think, yes, they're connected, and times I think no, they're not. They're linked because they're all people from the streets."

Meanwhile, Al Keller was making arrangements to bring Bill Corrigan to Saskatoon, making decisions about places and times, and working things out down to the minute. Their agent and informant was about to play the biggest role of his new career, and Keller wasn't taking anything for granted. Nothing was left to chance. Street rumours and witness accounts were one thing, but only words out of the killer's own mouth could guarantee a conviction.

Corrigan arrived in Saskatoon on Monday, January 9, 1995. Keller set him up in a safe room on 8th Street, far from the downtown core where there was too much chance of being recognized, or even spotted by Crawford, who was still making his usual rounds. For the next two days, Keller and other officers gave Corrigan a short course in the workings of the equipment, and did what they could to ease his anxiety levels, which were high at the best of times. No one was more aware than Bill Corrigan that his life might be in danger if John Crawford caught on to the scheme.

By Thursday night, the Mounties were ready to put their plan into action. Corrigan was installed in room 165 of the Imperial 400 Motel on Idylwyld Drive, a few blocks north of downtown Saskatoon. Microphones were concealed in strategic places around the room. Corrigan was fitted with a vest that carried an electronic microphone and transmitting device. He was also wearing a minuscule reel-to-reel tape recorder that fit into the small of his back and was connected to a microphone taped to his chest. Around the corner from the motel room, Constable Tom Steenvoorden, who had been assigned to the case a month earlier, was waiting in an unmarked vehicle with monitoring and recording equipment. Keller and other officers messed up the bed, filled the ashtrays with cigarette butts, and dropped a few pop cans around the room to give it that lived-in look. They were ready for a visit from John Crawford.

The tapes were rolling. Following his carefully prepared script, Bill Corrigan phoned John Martin Crawford and invited him to the motel for a reunion. It had been almost a year since the two men had been together, and Bill hadn't stopped to say good-bye before absconding with the bar receipts from the Albany. As he waited for Crawford to arrive, Corrigan paced the floor, talking to himself in short gasps. The pounding of his heart was audible in the monitoring devices.

Crawford arrived just before six o'clock. He knocked at the door. "Who is it?" Corrigan asked, pulling the door open as he spoke. "Geez, you driving that? Whose is it? What did you do, win a million-dollar lottery?"

Corrigan was evidently impressed with the sleek, dark grey 1986 Mercury Cougar John had arrived in. The car was definitely a step up from the old Nova Bill had spent so much time cruising in.

Crawford had more important things on his mind.

"You got Super Channel here? How come you don't have a room with food in it?"

Watching movies and eating junk food were John's two favourite pastimes, aside from sex.

Corrigan ordered food to the tune of $46, then got down to earning his pay. It didn't take much skill to lead Crawford into a conversation about the four murders near Saskatoon. Crawford can be heard clearly on the tape, his odd, choppy manner of speaking unmistakable: "There's only three that I did. There's another one"—referring to Janet Sylvestre—"you know that girl that testified against me. She's dead, but it wasn't me. Someone else."

Corrigan spoke in a squeaky voice, his nonstop chatter no doubt amusing to some who were listening and annoying to others. At one point he boasted that he was barred from the Albany Hotel because he had stolen $4,500 from the beer and wine store, then he turned the conversation back to the killings.

"You introduced that girl as Angie," Crawford said offhandedly.

"The one you did that night was sixteen," Corrigan replied.

"I thought she was at least twenty-two. But all the sperm and all that is gone." The conversation seemed to have no more significance to Crawford than if he had been discussing last night's hockey game with an old friend. "The one I'm worried about is the one with the blanket. I did nothing to her on the blanket. I covered her up. They found the cord, but they wouldn't find my fingerprints. I buried her about this much"—indicating two or three inches with thumb and forefingers—"others were just on top of the ground."

In the police vehicles outside, Al Keller and the other members of the GIS unit were ecstatic. They had heard John Crawford not only admit to three murders, but reveal holdback information that only the killer would have known. It could only get better.

In the room, Corrigan was saying, "I'm worried about my

knife being found. I'm marrying into this big Native family."

John wasn't interested. It was time to go for a drive. With the radio tuned to C-95, and Jennifer Warnes's cover of Leonard Cohen's "First We Take Manhattan" cranked up, the men drove up Idylwyld Drive. They stopped for coffee. The bill came to $2.03.

"I've got the three cents," Crawford offered generously.

Corrigan's body pack picked up every word as the men swapped stories and gossiped in the coffee shop. John bragged about a girl he had been seeing regularly until her boyfriend got suspicious.

"I always tell them I'm going to pay them after, then I don't. This one I can't do that to."

Back in the car, Crawford headed toward familiar turf, the 20th Street strip. For Corrigan, it was a trip down memory lane, and he was content to sit back and reminisce about driving the streets with John, looking for prostitutes. It was obvious to the electronic eavesdroppers that it was an activity the two men had enjoyed on numerous occasions.

"The little hookers used to hang around here, eh?" Corrigan piped up as Crawford drove by an arcade near Avenue G. "Remember that little redhead? Is that crazy bitch still around?"

They passed a small green house near the Lucky Horseshoe Bingo.

"There used to be two or three in there," Corrigan reminisced. "Good old 20th Street."

The banter continued for more than an hour, with both Crawford and Corrigan pointing out landmarks and observing the pedestrian traffic along the street. The second night provided more of the same fare, with Corrigan filling Crawford in on his imagined day's activities as Crawford checked out the motel room.

"This fold down to a bed?" he asked, pointing to a love seat. "What time did you order the chicken?"

Corrigan, more comfortable in his role, turned the conversation to Eva Taysup.

"That blanket wasn't taken from the Albany, was it?"

"No."

"Hope not, 'cause that'll come right back."

Corrigan changed the subject: "You won't believe who I ran into last night. Smiley's fucking sister. She asked me if I'd heard what happened to her sister. I was playing dumb."

"It wasn't me," said Crawford. "I was at home."

"Her and her boyfriend figure it was you or you know who did it."

Crawford had already admitted to killing three women. He would have little to lose by adding Janet Sylvestre to the list, but he steadfastly refused.

"I was shocked, too, when I heard it," he told Corrigan, leaving investigators to wonder if he was in fact telling the truth. The Sylvestre murder was practically a custom fit for John Martin Crawford. If he didn't do it, who did? If he did do it, why was he lying to a man he had already trusted with his most dreadful secrets?

Crawford left before nine o'clock that night in order to make his mother's curfew.

The RCMP added a new dimension to the next day's activities. They had finally released the name of the final victim, twenty-two-year-old Calinda Waterhen from around Loon Lake, Saskatchewan. The first remains to be discovered were the last to be identified, but it was a remarkable achievement by any measure. It had taken Ernie Walker and the RCMP investigators just 105 days to give names and histories to three anonymous skeletons.

The media reported the identification of Calinda Waterhen. Al Keller put a copy of the Saturday, January 14, edition of the *StarPhoenix* in room 165 at the Imperial 400 Motel.

"Did you see the fucking paper, John?" Corrigan shouted as Crawford came in. He didn't wait for an answer, but began reading it to him: "'The skeletal remains of the third young woman found south of the city in October has been identified. RCMP say the remains are those of Calinda Waterhen who would have been about twenty-two when she died . . .'"

"Don't worry." Crawford took the news in stride. "I'll take

the blame. Don't you worry. Just keep your mouth shut."

Corrigan flipped through the channels on the television, finally landing on a local station where the evening news was just beginning. After reporting a traffic accident on Warman Road, the news anchor turned to the Calinda Waterhen story. But Crawford had heard enough news.

"You got Super Channel on that?"

Corrigan, sounding panicky and agitated on the tape, was not about to let go of the subject. "Is there anything that could come back? Jimmy know anything?"—referring to Jimmy Mason—"because I know what he's like. I don't want him to know nothing."

Crawford reassured Corrigan that Mason would not be a factor: "It's just you and me. I got nothing to worry about and you got nothing to worry about."

Before long, John had other urges that needed attending to. Crawford and Corrigan got into the Cougar and headed to his familiar haunts. At Avenue O and 21st Street, directly behind St. Paul's Hospital, Crawford stopped to chat with a prostitute.

"We'll give you $20 for each of us," John offered.

The young woman peered into the window to check out his companion. "What about thirty each? You guys got rubbers?"

"No," John replied. "But I can't have kids and neither can he. My name's Joseph. What's yours?"

"I'm Barb."

"I'm Bill," Corrigan piped up from the passenger seat. Nobody heard him.

"Tell her your name," said John.

"I did."

"She didn't hear you."

"It's Todd," said Bill.

Barb soon decided that it would probably be worth her while to accompany "Joseph" and "Bill/Todd" back to their motel. Once there, Corrigan realized that the tape on his reel-to-reel was running out. He took the opportunity to leave the room while John and Barb had sex. The two wasted no time removing their clothes. The hidden mikes picked up the sounds of the bed creaking and Crawford's desultory conversation with the young prostitute as he satisfied his appetite.

Corrigan ran to the RCMP van to change the tape. Moments later John and the prostitute had finished their business. John emerged from the room as Corrigan came running back. The timing couldn't have been better.

It was Corrigan's turn. Clearly, he had no intention of stripping down in front of the woman and revealing all his concealed electronic devices. He chose instead to give her a warning: "Don't ever go out with him alone."

Sex acts and wise counsel completed, the men agreed to take Barb to a bingo hall at 22nd Street and Avenue W. Then they returned to the motel. On the way, Bill said: "I told you last night we'd get something. We got our oil changed, and $40 isn't that bad."

"We had to hunt for her, though," Crawford complained.

Back at the motel, Corrigan was eager to tie up some loose ends. He wanted to make sure that his friend had implicated himself irrevocably.

"Why did you take them to the same place, John?" he asked, conversationally.

"I drove them out there, dragged the bodies into the bushes. After the first one . . . it was the safest place."

At Corrigan's prompting, Crawford admitted that he had killed Eva Taysup by a cement factory near Avenue P and 11th Street. It was a place he often took prostitutes. It was bleak, cold, and ugly, not the sort of place a man would usually take a woman, or where a woman would go if she weren't in need of money.

"She was going to yell rape. I choked her."

"You've got more balls than a brass monkey," said Corrigan, both misusing and mutilating the familiar winter metaphor.

"This one here"—pointing to the photograph of Calinda Waterhen in the *StarPhoenix*—"I did it at the bushes, hit her over the head. We were sniffing."

Finally, Crawford admitted that he had used a knife—Bill Corrigan's knife—to kill Shelley Napope. Then it was time to wrap up the evening. Crawford's curfew was fast approaching. The men discussed plans for Sunday.

"I'll phone you, but I won't use my name," Corrigan promised as Crawford got up to leave. Victoria Crawford didn't like her son's friends calling, and she had a particular dislike for Corrigan, whom she regarded as a bad influence.

As Crawford pulled away, Corrigan unleashed a sudden stream of profanity. Perhaps it was just a release of tension, but it certainly cast more heat than light on his personal feelings for the man he had in all likelihood just sent to jail for the rest of his life. "Yes, yes, beautiful!" he yelled. "I don't care what anybody says, it's been a beautiful fucking night! Scum bucket! Prick thinks he's so fucking good!"

He calmed down. "Okay," he said to the listening officers, "he's on his way home. I hope you guys got everything."

The equipment was turned off just after 9:00 PM on Saturday, January 14, 1995.

Confident they now had all they needed to take the file to Crown prosecutor Terry Hinz, Sergeant Colin Crocker's team made plans to arrest Crawford. Yet on Tuesday, January 17, three days after John Crawford had virtually confessed to three murders, Crocker announced that, since all three remains had been identified, the focus of the investigation had shifted. "If all the evidence comes to fact," he told the *StarPhoenix*, he hoped they would "be able to solve this. But right now we're still grasping for straws." Nonetheless, he had high praise for Dr. Ernie Walker and his own officers, particularly Constable Wayne Wiebe, who followed up uncountable leads and obtained the dental records.

Five days after the motel operation, the Mounties moved in.

For the better part of the past four months, the RCMP surveillance team had been trailing John Martin Crawford. On Thursday, January 19, they watched him leave his mother's group home on Avenue Q North and head for his favourite territory, the hooker stroll along 21st Street. Eight officers were in the area, awaiting orders to bring this part of the operation to a close. They wanted Crawford in a place they felt was relatively secure before they moved in.

In the end, it was anticlimactic, even laughable. A marked RCMP cruiser cut Crawford off on Avenue M South. Crawford slammed on the brakes. Al Keller, who had been tailing Crawford, was out of his own car in seconds and standing by the driver's side window of Victoria Crawford's Cougar. Crawford made no effort to resist as Keller slipped the handcuffs over his wrists. Keller read Crawford his rights and informed him that he was being charged with three counts of first-degree murder in connection with the deaths of Shelley Napope, Eva Taysup, and Calinda Waterhen. Incredibly, all Crawford wanted to know was who supplied the prisoners' meals, McDonalds or Burger King, and would he be in the cells in time for supper? Since it was just after six o'clock, he would indeed be in time for supper, the first of thousands he would enjoy at taxpayers' expense.

Chapter Four

RÉSUMÉ OF A SERIAL KILLER

*"Their only way of relating is through
humiliating and destroying their victims."*

—Elliott Leyton

By any of the accepted definitions, John Martin Crawford qual-
ifies as that most heinous of multiple murderers, a serial killer.

According to one definition, a serial killer is any murderer
who commits more than one random slaying, with a break
between crimes. Other authorities speak of a string of random
killings with an emotional cooling-off period between each crime.
The most common and widely accepted definition, and the one
usually credited to the FBI, characterizes a serial killer as someone who commits three or more unrelated killings separated by a
cooling-off period and involving sadistic sexual violence.

The crimes John Martin Crawford has committed over the
past two decades place him in the company of such notorious
killers as David Berkowitz, New York City's "Son of Sam," the

charming and deadly Ted Bundy, New Brunswick's Michael Wayne McGray,* and Canada's worst offender, the child-killer Clifford Olson.

Crawford's résumé begins in Lethbridge, Alberta, where he killed thirty-five-year-old Mary Jane Serloin in 1981. Just nineteen at the time, Crawford was originally charged with first-degree murder, but was sentenced to a mere ten years in prison when he agreed to plead guilty to manslaughter. The young killer was given day parole after five years, broke the terms of his release, and was promptly returned to prison. There he stayed until March 23, 1989, when he was again set free, this time under what was known at the time as mandatory supervision. While living at home with his mother, Victoria Crawford, John managed to avoid prison, but he didn't stay out of trouble. In December 1990, for example, he was fined $250 for trying to hire a prostitute. By 1992, the year his ten-year sentence expired, he was a walking time bomb. He sniffed solvents, went on drinking binges, and regularly took intravenous drugs. It was not uncommon for him to consume twenty-four beer and a twenty-six-ounce bottle of hard liquor over the course of a day. That was the year he murdered Calinda Waterhen, Shelley Napope, and Eva Taysup. The RCMP suspect he may also have killed two other women, either that year or late in 1991: Shirley Lonethunder and Cynthia Baldhead have not been seen for almost nine years. Crawford must also be considered a suspect in the 1994 death of Janet Sylvestre.

In their comprehensive examination of serial killing, *The A to Z Encyclopedia of Serial Killers*, Harold Schechter and David Everitt note that North American society has become obsessed with the phenomenon:

> For all the genuine horror and revulsion they inspire in us, there's no point in denying that

---

* *McGray has been convicted of three murders at the time of writing but claims to have killed sixteen people.*

serial killers exert a dark attraction. They appeal not just to our morbid interest but also to our need to comprehend an ultimate human mystery: how people who seem so ordinary, so much like the rest of us, can possess the hearts and minds of monsters.

True crime books have been around for centuries, but it is only in the past few years that the public has embraced the serial killing genre with such unabashed enthusiasm. It was that morbid fascination that led to the appearance of Jeffrey Dahmer, the homosexual cannibal from Milwaukee, on the cover of *People* magazine in 1991. Names such as Bundy, Berkowitz, and Olson, as well as John Wayne Gacy, Albert DeSalvo (the Boston Strangler), and Henry Lee Lucas have become household words. Indeed, an entire industry has sprung up, essentially venerating the exploits of these most flamboyant and appalling of killers. A number of American companies are marketing serial-killer trading cards, while others offer comic books, T-shirts, and even dishes cast from an actual human skull.

A more erudite examination of the subject, *Hunting Humans: The Rise of the Modern Multiple Murderer*, by Canadian anthropologist Elliott Leyton, was first published in 1986. To this day, the book disappears off store shelves by the thousands, not only in North America but worldwide, in countries such as Poland and Japan where retailers have been hard-pressed to keep up with the demand for Dr. Leyton's book.

That John Martin Crawford has not become a household name even in his home province of Saskatchewan is somewhat perplexing. This is, after all, a man who savagely raped and killed at least four women, yet he remains virtually unknown in the world of crime. He is an enigma—a multiple murderer who shuns the publicity that his criminal colleagues usually crave.

Crawford does, however, share many of the other traits common to serial killers. FBI Special Agent Robert Ressler has identified several general characteristics of serial sex-murderers:

- over 90 percent of them are white males
- their families often have criminal, psychiatric, and alcoholic histories
- they are commonly abused—psychologically, physically, and sexually—as children. Sometimes, the abuser is a stranger. Sometimes, it is a friend. Often, it is a family member.
- many of them have spent time in institutions as children and have records of early psychiatric problems
- they have a high rate of suicide attempts

The list, contained in Schechter and Everitt's *Encyclopedia of Serial Killers*, also suggests that many serial killers are intelligent, with IQs in the "bright normal" range. Clearly, John Crawford does not fit this criterion. References to his low intelligence and learning difficulties appear in a number of professional assessments. It is a criterion that Elliott Leyton disputes, in any case: "People think of these people as being clever," he says. "They are very rarely that. Their only way of relating is through humiliating and destroying their victims." Dr. Leyton has observed, further, that serial killers often take out their anger against a specific social class, preying on the most vulnerable members of that class.

Virtually everything journalists know about John Martin Crawford has been gleaned from court records—bulging file folders and cardboard boxes filled with psychiatric reports, affidavits from the killer and his mother, witness statements, and other documents prepared in advance of bail hearings or other court appearances. Court testimony provides the merest glimpse of the man behind the murders. His lawyers, Mark Brayford and Hugh Harradence, opted not to present any evidence on behalf of their client at his triple-murder trial in 1996. Crawford did not utter a word prior to his sentencing. This silence was interpreted by the trial judge, Mr. Justice David Wright, as evidence of a lack of remorse on the part of a heartless killer who would offer no explanation for his actions. John Crawford and his mother have both consistently rejected requests for interviews.

Many of the early psychiatric reports are based on the briefest of interviews that took place as Crawford was moved from one facility to the next. He has been assessed dozens of times over the years, and appears to be candid only when it serves his current purpose. On occasion, he has described his childhood as happy; other times he has talked of miserable years struggling with his studies and fighting with other children on the playground.

John was born in Steinbach, Manitoba, on March 29, 1962. The birth was difficult, but mother and son survived with no lasting physical damage. The mother was twenty-one and unmarried. In 1964 she married Al Crawford, and a stepbrother was born. A sister arrived in 1967 after the family had moved to Vancouver. Al was a taxi driver with alcohol problems. He and Victoria were divorced in the mid-1980s, while John was serving his sentence for manslaughter in the death of Mary Jane Serloin.

When John was four years old, he suffered burns to his upper chest, neck, and arm as the result of playing with a cigarette lighter. He spent several days in hospital and emerged with extensive scarring that left him open to teasing from other children. The incident occurred while young John was in the care of a babysitter. It was by no means the only trauma he suffered while under the care of babysitters; notably, he was sexually molested at the age of four, and again at age seven.

As a five-year-old attending kindergarten, John was told that he was stupid, and his teachers recommended that he be transferred to another school for grade one. Sometimes quiet and withdrawn, sometimes hyperactive and disruptive, John, to no one's surprise, failed grade one. At home, Victoria was fighting a self-admitted addiction to bingo while her husband, Al, fought his own losing battle with alcohol and regularly gambled away his earnings as a cab driver. Beginning at the age of three, John ran away repeatedly. The police were often called to find the youngster and bring him home.

The Crawfords realized eventually that their troubled son needed professional help. He was sent to psychologists at Vancouver General Hospital as a result of his behavioural problems and poor academic performance. The boy was experiencing nightmares as well, and he was deathly afraid of the dark. By the time he was twelve, he had developed into a bully, often picking on smaller children. He had also found a way of dealing with his mounting personal problems: he became a glue sniffer.

In a secluded place in a park or in the country, he would settle down to a ritualistic, almost spiritual session of substance abuse. The ritual included food and drink. John would talk to himself, to the glue, to the bag he was going to squirt it into to get more comprehensive coverage while inhaling, and to any other paraphernalia he might find necessary as the occasion demanded. He discussed his expectations both with himself and with the inanimate objects around him, anticipating visions of green grass, swaying trees, majestic mountains, and placid lakes. Baptized a Catholic, John later became disenchanted with a religion based on "how much money a person can make." Nonetheless, he occasionally had religious experiences, particularly when he was away from the city. He once told an addictions counsellor that his most meaningful religious beliefs were the traditional Native ones.

"I don't feel so alone when I offer up a token to the Indians' god," he said in 1992.

The glue sniffing, which Victoria remembers occurring on a daily basis, led to other problems. He ran away from home, he stole cars, he fought with the police. As he entered his teens, he began to drink and use street drugs such as marijuana, LSD, hallucinogenic mushrooms, and prescription medications including Valium, Ritalin, and Talwin.

At the Saskatchewan Penitentiary in 1996, he told a staff member from the Mental Health Unit of his first sexual encounter, which he shared with two other boys and an eleven-year-old girl. They paid the girl $5 to have sex with them. He was just thirteen at the time. Later he recalled visiting "sex booths" to watch "sex shows." Sex, he came to understand, was something women provided for a fee. He had no reason to believe otherwise.

In a 1998 interview with Stanley Semrau, a Kelowna forensic psychiatrist, John admitted that he had begun hearing voices at about the age of sixteen, voices that continued to torment him.

A report prepared by Dr. Semrau prior to Crawford's appeal in 1999 contained the following description of the voices:

> Most of the time he just heard voices, but he recalls on one occasion having an apparent brief visual hallucination of two green ladies, naked from the waist up, whom he believes were the source of the voices. He says that the voices would often tell him to do bad things such as "kill that person, they're bothering you" or to do other things such as commit property crimes. He recalls the women's voices also simply advising him on his behaviour such as "you should get dressed—you shouldn't be naked" or "you shouldn't go out with that girl—she isn't attractive." The voices would sometimes tell him to hurt people or to kiss women and he recalls once acting on that advice and being charged with assault.

According to a rationale that was uniquely his own, John determined that the voices came from UFOs or other planets. He generally heard their commands while he was intoxicated, but occasionally he heard them even after he had been clean for several days. When they did speak to him while intoxicated, he felt like "a stronger, better person," more capable of engaging in aggressive behaviour. Dr. Semrau wrote:

> He was once told to run over someone with his car or told to smash a store window with his car and steal a rifle. He also resisted commands to commit suicide. He recalls that he would be more likely to obey the voices if he were intoxicated.

Crawford admitted to Dr. Semrau that he had lied to Saskatoon psychiatrist Karl Oberdieck when he said that he had not heard the voices for two years. John had disliked the powerful antipsychotics he had been taking and hoped Dr. Oberdieck would not prescribe any more if he were no longer hearing the voices.

During four hours of interviews conducted over two days at the penitentiary in Prince Albert in 1998, Dr. Semrau pushed hard to learn if the voices had been a factor in the 1981 killing of Mary Jane Serloin or in the three murders of 1992. But "even with repeated careful questioning in this area," the doctor wrote, "he was adamant that none of these homicides were in any way associated with hearing voices or any other apparent psychotic symptoms." The psychiatrist went on to note some of the inconsistencies in the psychiatric history he had been provided with prior to meeting Crawford:

> Problems noted at various times have included limited intelligence, possible dyslexia, severe substance abuse, and intermittent findings of psychosis or schizophrenia. In terms of schizophrenia or other psychotic diagnoses, there has been considerable inconsistency in the psychiatric diagnoses over the years. It may be that at least some of this inconsistency is explained by Mr. Crawford's admission that he had at times untruthfully denied hearing voices in order to avoid treatment with antipsychotic medications. This is not an unusual experience in ordinary clinical practice with many patients.

In the early years of his ten-year sentence for manslaughter, John Crawford had difficulty coping. He felt threatened in prison, and his anxiety led to self-mutilation and other bizarre behaviour. Originally sent to the federal institution at Drumheller, Alberta, he was later transferred to Prince Albert, and was several times sent from there to the Regional Psychiatric Centre in Saskatoon. One such visit took place in April 1984, a few months after he had slashed a wrist in the hope of being placed in segregation. At the psych centre, a staff psychiatrist reviewed Crawford's history and concluded that the "cheerful" man before him was "quite co-operative and friendly . . . and does not show any evidence of formal psychiatric disorder." The doctor determined that Crawford was of average intelligence but seemed to experience difficulty reading and spelling. As for the murder of Mary Jane Serloin, "He denies having raped the victim and I do not see him as a sex offender." The psychiatrist presumably had some difficulty reading as well, otherwise he could not have failed to note that Mary Jane's breasts had been mutilated by deep bite marks— indisputably inflicted by Crawford—during an event that Lethbridge police immediately labelled a sexual attack.

A year later, Crawford was back at the Regional Psychiatric Centre after a psychotic interlude in the exercise yard of the Prince Albert Penitentiary. Described as being "acutely disoriented, behaving idiotically, throwing sticks about, smearing toothpaste over himself and laughing inappropriately," Crawford blamed his condition on a can of tainted salmon he had eaten three months earlier.

At the centre, his speech was frequently incomprehensible, and he stared vacantly for long periods. Even his mother noticed something was wrong. During her regular visits he giggled without reason and often could not understand what she was saying or recall earlier conversations. His behaviour frightened staff and patients alike. He hid knives in his room, but denied having done so when the weapons were discovered. He jumped behind other patients to scare them. He heard voices. He claimed to have ESP.

A psychiatrist reviewing Crawford's file in 1985 noted that the patient had previously been diagnosed with a personality disorder and had a history of substance abuse. "It is possible that he has been suffering from a drug induced psychosis," the doctor concluded in his report, "but I consider the more likely diagnosis to be that of an early hebephrenic schizophrenic illness." (Hebephrenic schizophrenia can include periods of acute silliness, delusions, and hallucinations.)

After violating his parole conditions in 1987, Crawford was returned to the prison at Drumheller. It was there on February 23, 1988, that he met Dr. V. Singh, a staff psychiatrist from the Regional Psychiatric Centre in Saskatoon. As numerous mental health professionals had done before him and would do again in the future, Dr. Singh dutifully recorded John Martin Crawford's criminal record and family history, noting that he was

> exposed to illicit drugs and alcohol at an early age . . . [For] his present charges [killing Mary Jane Serloin] he underwent a psychiatric assessment for his pretrial report [and] a diagnosis of antisocial personality disorder was made. Investigations which included skull x-ray, EEG, did not reveal any abnormalities.

Dr. Singh learned, further, that Crawford had become proficient with a sewing machine, and was enjoying this new activity.

> He marketed this particular skill while in the Saskatchewan Penitentiary and plans to make it one of his means for livelihood. He has been attending Alcoholics Anonymous, social, life, and communication skills programs on a regular basis and strongly believes he has gained enough insight into his problems.
>
> On mental state examination he presented as a cooperative, conversant and plausible man who spoke freely, apparently frankly, of his past and present life history. His physical health was good and there appeared to be no evidence of any formal psychiatric illness. He was correctly oriented in time, place, and persona and his higher cognitive functions were well within normal limits.
>
> In summation, the writer could find no evidence of any major psychiatric disorder, hence no useful medical recommendation was made in this case other than he continue working on his problem areas through various structured programs available to him at his parent institution.

In a psychiatric parole report prepared in November 1988, four months before Crawford was scheduled to be released, Regional Psychiatric Centre staff psychiatrist Dr. W. A. Botros had grave reservations about John's ability to return successfully to the community. The young man with the vague responses had serious mental issues, Dr. Botros determined.

> This is very likely a case of schizophrenia with heavy load on the negative symptomatology. This means that the condition started at a young age and led to a great degree of handicap for the individual. The recovery with medications tends to be limited and the prognosis on a whole is moderate to poor.

Dr. Botros's concerns were tempered somewhat by his perhaps optimistic regard for Victoria Crawford, who was anxious to have her son return to live with her and help with the operation of her group home.

> She is a very capable person in looking after some of the psychiatric patients in the community. She runs her own private nursing home for a number of patients, some of whom have been released from the penitentiary system with mental illness. She is undoubtedly very successful in maintaining a big majority of them out of trouble. Mrs. Crawford seems to be very keen on the idea of her son returning to live with her. She feels that with new changes in the group home she runs, John would be able to have a peaceful life without too much hassle. She attributed his previous failure in maintaining his conditions of parole to the fact that the place was crowded and her own quarters had very little privacy.
> It is undoubtedly a great advantage to Crawford to have such access to a place where he

could be monitored closely if any condition of probation has been granted.

Dr. Botros noted that visiting psychiatrists to the Regional Psychiatric Centre had diagnosed Crawford as a schizophrenic, an opinion he agreed with, adding that Crawford's particular condition was "one of the least favourable forms of schizophrenia in terms of prognosis." On release, Botros concluded, Crawford would require "very close monitoring of his drinking and drug abuse by a variety of chemical tests."

Four months later, while Crawford was being held at the psych centre awaiting release on mandatory supervision, a colleague of Dr. Singh and Dr. Botros issued a clear warning. "Since Crawford suffers from schizophrenia and has a long history of delinquent behaviour," wrote Dr. R. Denson, "there is a high probability that he will become involved in further crimes."

Once back on the street and in the care of Victoria Crawford, who had never actually demonstrated much ability to control her son, John Crawford was placed under the care of Saskatoon psychiatrist Karl Oberdieck. Dr. Oberdieck gradually discontinued all antipsychotic medications. John responded reasonably well, he observed, but lacked motivation.

Throughout the remainder of 1989 and most of 1990, John Martin Crawford seems to have made a reasonable readjustment to society. In December 1990 he tried to hire a prostitute who turned out to be an undercover cop. For another year after that, though, he appears to have maintained a low profile.

The year 1992 would demonstrate beyond a doubt that, despite the numerous psychiatric assessments and programs he had undergone while in prison, John Crawford remained a very dangerous and sick man. He needed help in 1992, more help than Victoria Crawford and all the addictions counsellors, psychiatrists, and Justice officials in Saskatchewan could deliver.

Chapter Five

A MOTHER'S LOVE

"I can't believe it. He's a good boy."

—Victoria Crawford, 1995

The one constant in the troubled, violent life of John Martin Crawford has been the obsessive loyalty of his mother, Victoria Crawford, a diminutive woman who stands less than 150 centimetres (5′) tall. In the face of the most damning and horrific evidence to the contrary, she has remained steadfast in her belief in her son's innocence. Victoria Crawford did not ask "Why did he *do* these things?" but rather "Why did he *say* these things?" after hearing her son describe with chilling detachment how he had killed a woman, wrapped her corpse in a blanket, and covered her with leaves and branches. "A normal person doesn't do that," she said.

Indeed.

Fourteen years after John Martin Crawford attacked and killed Mary Jane Serloin in Lethbridge, he was arrested in

Saskatoon and charged with three further killings. Victoria Crawford seemed to have completely sublimated the previous incident and the subsequent incarceration of her son for the better part of a decade when she spoke to *StarPhoenix* reporter Terry Craig on the telephone the night John was arrested.

"I can't believe it," she said. "He's a good boy."

These words were uttered by a woman whose nineteen-year-old son had been convicted of manslaughter on the basis of tooth marks on the victim's breasts that matched his dental impressions. By a woman whose son, since his release from the Saskatchewan Penitentiary in 1989, had been charged with aggravated assault and sexual assault, and spent months in jail, either in remand awaiting trial or serving time. By a woman whose son had been in trouble with the police in virtually every city they lived in since the time he was twelve.

Again, most of what is known about the relationship between John Crawford and his mother has been gleaned from the mountain of psychiatric assessments and reports penned by alcohol and drug counsellors and other authorities who have interviewed John and, on occasion, Victoria, during the course of her son's difficulties with the law. Victoria refuses to talk to the media since John's arrest. The two sentences she gave to the *StarPhoenix* reporter when John was arrested in 1995 were a rare exception, and she hung up immediately afterward.

Victoria Crawford made the news in 1989 when she was the subject of a story involving the provincial Rentalsman's Office and her unsuccessful efforts to evict a tenant from a revenue property she owned. She came across in the story as feisty and determined but that is the only glimpse the public has had of her. At John's preliminary hearing and later at the trial, Victoria arrived alone, parked her car—the same 1986 Cougar that her son had used to pick up women on his nightly rounds—and entered the buildings by herself: the provincial courthouse in the spring of 1995 and the Queen's Bench Court for the trial in 1996. With neither friends nor relatives to accompany her, the tiny woman set her eyes directly ahead and walked quickly into court, dismissing all requests for interviews.

Victoria and her eldest son were always close. Many of her life decisions have been made with John's welfare uppermost in her mind. When four-year-old John was badly burned in the lighter incident and Victoria learned that the disfiguring burns to her son's neck and chest required medical attention not available in Manitoba, the family moved to Vancouver where John could receive specialized treatment. Fifteen years later, when John was convicted of manslaughter and sent to the Saskatchewan Penitentiary at Prince Albert, Victoria moved from Lethbridge to Saskatoon to be closer to him. On visiting day, she would take the bus to Prince Albert, 145 kilometres north of Saskatoon, then walk several kilometres, often in bone-chilling winter weather, to the maximum security prison on the outskirts of the city.

On the night John was arrested for murder, Victoria called Mark Brayford, one of Saskatoon's most prominent lawyers. The highly skilled Brayford doesn't come cheap. Neither is he inclined to arrange payment schedules for his clients. When he quoted $25,000 to handle John's preliminary hearing, Victoria came up with the money. As the preliminary hearing approached, Victoria decided that John needed more help than Brayford could offer, and she called Hugh Harradence in Prince Albert. She wanted Hugh, the son of legendary Prince Albert defence lawyer Clyne Harradence, to assist Brayford in representing her son. The meter was running as soon as he agreed. He quoted her fees of $800 per day, $500 per half day, and $75 per hour for research and preparation. For his role in the preliminary hearing, he agreed to limit his fees to a maximum of $10,000. Victoria immediately sent a retainer of $5,000, promising to pay another $2,500 on the opening day of the preliminary hearing. Harradence's bill for the hearing came in at $6,518. When John was committed to stand trial Brayford required another $25,000. Harradence estimated his fees at $16,000, assuming the trial didn't go beyond two weeks. In the unlikely event that it did, he would charge $1,500 per additional day. The money arrived in plenty of time for the trial.

The fees quoted by Brayford and Harradence fell well within the bounds of normal compensation for a murder case that is being privately funded rather than through legal aid. But Victoria had other expenses to meet as well. One of these was for a private investigator hired by Brayford to dig up some dirt on Bill Corrigan in an attempt to discredit him as a witness at the murder trial. The investigator's fees came to just over $4,000.

By the conclusion of the trial, Victoria Crawford had spent almost $80,000 in legal fees, taxes, and disbursements. And unsuccessful appeal bids added a few thousand more to the tab as she continued to pay legal fees in the vain hope of keeping her son out of jail.

Virtually all the reports of the various mental health professionals who examined John Crawford refer to his mother's desperate efforts to obtain help for her son's array of problems. For the better part of twenty years, Victoria sought treatment for John's addictions. In 1992 alone she took him to half a dozen treatment centres throughout Saskatchewan, but none of the facilities was able to reverse the pattern of substance abuse—a pattern that appears to have fuelled his appetite for sexual gratification and violence.

It is natural for parents to defend their children, to blame someone else if they get in trouble at school or with the law, to search for bad influences that might be leading them to act out certain behaviours that seem out of character. But Victoria Crawford has taken this natural inclination to a point far beyond this.

Dr. Robin Menzies, a Saskatoon psychiatrist, is familiar with the phenomenon of parental love that goes beyond reasonable bounds. In a thirty-year career that includes a period as director of the Regional Psychiatric Centre in Saskatoon, an institution that houses federal and provincial inmates with a wide range of mental problems, sexual dysfunctions, and addictions, he has encountered it more than once. But he is baffled by the degree of loyalty Victoria Crawford has demonstrated toward her son, a four-time convicted killer.

Dr. Menzies characterizes the relationship between Victoria and John Crawford as "an abnormal interaction between child and parent." The doctor believes that Victoria Crawford's "inability to accept what she has heard" speaks volumes about her.

John's below-average intelligence and his abnormal physical and emotional requirements, which were first manifested at a very young age, seem to have combined with Victoria's passion for meeting her son's every need to create an exceptional bond between mother and son. Victoria Crawford might be carrying a burden of guilt based on childhood events that may have damaged her son emotionally, or she may simply—and not unnaturally—be unable to face the possibility that her reputation in the community would be significantly diminished as a consequence of being recognized as the mother of a serial killer. But whatever her motives, according to Menzies, "she is taking it to an extreme."

In a two-and-a-half-hour interview with Dr. Stanley Semrau in 1998, the British Columbia psychiatrist who also interviewed John at length, Victoria Crawford presented a point of view that diverged dramatically from the reality of her son's life.

> Mrs. Crawford indicates that she was never aware of John behaving violently and [he] tended to be virtually always peaceful or even somewhat withdrawn. She indicates he was never aggressive or assaultive with her whatever and the only time she has seen aggressive behaviour is when John protected her from one of her boarders who was assaulting her. Mrs. Crawford recalls feeling that John generally had positive and respectful attitudes towards women and seemed to treat them well, including a woman he dated for about a year in 1993. She was aware that he went out with prostitutes at times and noted that he seemed to have an essentially neutral

attitude toward them, not looking down on them or expressing negative feelings towards them.

Mrs. Crawford indicated that John had never told her anything about the killings due to lack of privacy for conversations in prison and indicated that she found it hard to believe that he could carry out such killings due to his non-violent nature and expressed the belief that he must have been intoxicated to have done any such thing.

"It was clear," Dr. Semrau concluded charitably, "that Mrs. Crawford viewed her son in a more positive light than might be objectively justifiable, in part because it appeared she was unaware of considerable problematic behaviour in which John had engaged in over the years."

From Victoria Crawford's perspective as a loving, forgiving, if somewhat forgetful mother, it was Bill Corrigan's malevolent influence that led to the problems her son began having in 1992. Until Corrigan got out of prison in late 1991, according to Victoria, John was not only abstaining from substance abuse but also earning his keep by doing chores around the group home. She firmly believes that Corrigan is the cause of John's descent into greater substance abuse, violent outbursts, and, ultimately, multiple murder.

Victoria was first introduced to Corrigan in May 1992. "Bill Corrigan seemed to have a lot of power over John, who is not very smart," she later recalled. "I began to worry more about John and took him to medical places to get help." Corrigan belittled John, she said, encouraging his erratic behaviour.

Corrigan and Crawford were constant drinking companions in the summer of 1992, but it is difficult to determine who was the leader and who was the follower. To be sure, Bill Corrigan was a disreputable character; by that point in his life, he had spent the better part of two decades behind bars. But how much influence he had on John Crawford is debatable. John was more than capable of wreaking mayhem on his own.

On May 9, 1992, Janet Sylvestre reported to the police that she had been raped by Crawford in a house across the street from Victoria Crawford's group home on Avenue Q North. Crawford denied the charge. His recollection of the events following the alleged assault include a beating he received himself at the hands of muggers at the Albany Hotel and the loss both of his wallet and a friend's car. He told a psychiatrist that he was confused for the next few hours before being arrested. He appeared in court on Monday, May 11. Guilty or not, his federal sentence did not expire for another month, and he wasn't going anywhere. He stayed in remand until June 18; two days after his ten-year sentence for the killing of Mary Jane Serloin officially ended. It was then that Victoria Crawford put up cash bail of $4,000 and, after agreeing to a host of conditions, including a 10:30 PM curfew and a promise to refrain from drinking, John was released into his mother's custody. A preliminary hearing was set for November.

But in the summer of 1992, John Martin Crawford wasn't capable of following any court-imposed conditions. He was out of control, a danger to himself and to anyone he came in contact with. By August, Victoria was beside herself with worry. On the 4th, after several days of sniffing paint thinner and bingeing on beer and marijuana, a shaky, perspiring John Crawford arrived at Royal University Hospital. He was depressed, he complained, and he hadn't been sleeping well for two weeks. His speech was slurred, often nonsensical. He stared into corners. He took an instrument from an emergency room table and announced that he wanted to listen to music. He mistook a book for a telephone.

By mid-afternoon, a psychiatric consultant had decided that Larson House, a facility for the short-term treatment for alcoholics, was the appropriate place for John Crawford. It was the wrong decision. Once at Larson House, John began spilling hot coffee and tearing up a set of hockey cards that he found on a coffee table. Mumbling and confused, he was promptly loaded into an ambulance and driven downtown to City Hospital, where he was admitted to the psychiatric ward. Two days later, he was released and referred back to Larson House.

The next day, the saga of John Martin Crawford very nearly came to an end when RCMP officers found him semi-comatose in the Bare Ass Beach area south of the city. He was wearing a T-shirt and socks, and nothing else. He was badly sunburnt, and running a fever of 110 degrees Fahrenheit. He was pronounced dead on arrival at St. Paul's Hospital, the third Saskatoon hospital he had visited that week, but emergency staff managed to revive him. At St. Paul's, it was decided that John should be sent to the detox centre at the Melfort Union Hospital, a two-hour drive from Saskatoon. Karl Oberdieck, who had treated John previously, happened to be in attendance at St. Paul's, and felt that the Melfort centre would be a good starting point for a long-term treatment strategy. Dr. Oberdieck also believed that it was time to wean John from his mother's influence. Discharging him from St. Paul's after four days, Oberdieck wrote:

> It is my feeling at this stage that John would probably not be best to return to his mom since she is over-protective and has a long-standing severe problem in dealing with John who has a very serious problem and it may not be the best for John to return home since his mom is quite unknowledgeable in how to help him.

Dr. Oberdieck's remarks shed quite a different light on Dr. Botros's earlier comments that John was fortunate to have a mother who was capable of dealing with psychiatric patients.

Staff at the detox centre found him co-operative and compliant, although an addiction counsellor formed the opinion that he was a bit of a braggart and tended to be a manipulator. John was not as slow as he liked to make out, the Melfort staff suspected. Moreover, they found "no evidence of schizophrenia, but rather more of a sociopathic personality disorder." He was discharged after four days.

Two days after leaving Melfort, Crawford was admitted to

St. Joseph's Hospital in Estevan, a small city in southeastern Saskatchewan. At St. Joe's, he spoke at length about his glue sniffing and other addictions, claiming that they were motivated by feelings of isolation from the rest of the world. He told counsellors that he was looking forward to a treatment program that would provide alternatives to his drug and alcohol abuse. He spoke of a life that would see him with a job, a wife, and some responsibility. "I have only thirty to fifty years of life left," he told one counsellor, "and I would rather live them healthy and free than inside a jail cell." He acknowledged that his self-esteem had hit rock bottom: "I feel like a wimp; it's like taking off a leather jacket and only having bare skin left."

Perhaps it was a rare moment of self-knowledge in Estevan that allowed him to recognize that he was in deep trouble and desperately needed help. More often, he fought with staff members and other patients, and once with a male patient over the affections of a female patient. Through August and into the next month, Crawford also visited the Regina detox centre and the Angus Campbell Treatment Centre in Moose Jaw. Nowhere, it seemed, did he fit in or find the help he needed.

Between court-supported forays into various treatment centres, John cheerfully ignored the conditions of his release into the bail supervision program. A random curfew check at 11:11 PM on August 27 revealed that he was not at home and his mother had no idea where he was. On October 2 the bail order became moot when he was charged with attempted murder after he savagely beat a Saskatoon man, Derek Langager, after the latter refused to give him a cigarette.

At the preliminary hearing on November 30, Provincial Court Judge Albert Lavoie ruled that there was insufficient evidence to send Crawford to trial on the attempted murder charge. There was, however, enough evidence to proceed with the lesser charge of aggravated assault. Two days later Crawford made a pitch to be released until the trial, which was scheduled for the spring. But this time, despite Victoria Crawford's offer to come up with a further $2,000 bail, John was staying put. Bail Supervision Officer Brian Campbell had written a strongly worded report detailing Crawford's previous transgressions, and warning of the "high possibility that he will continue to re-offend." The judge agreed, and Crawford was returned to the remand unit at the Saskatoon Correctional Centre to await trial in June 1993. On the appointed day, June 22, Court of Queen's Bench Justice A. L. Sirois convicted Crawford of aggravated assault and sentenced him to one year in the provincial correctional centre. Crawford, guards at the jail say, did his time quietly, satisfying his voracious appetite for food and sex by eating and masturbating more or less constantly in his cell.

The attack on Derek Langager, frightening as it undoubtedly was to the victim, had the salutary result of temporarily removing a serial killer from the streets of Saskatoon. But by then three women, at least, were already dead.

"Oh shit—nailed for another murder," he thought after Eva Taysup slumped lifelessly onto the seat of his mother's car. He had wrung her neck. Not long afterward—quite possibly the next night, if Crawford's recollection is accurate—he throttled Calinda Waterhen in a similar fashion after the couple had had sex. His reaction? "Fuck, here goes another one."

Remorse was not something John Martin Crawford experienced. His victims were disposable. The problems they caused could be dealt with simply by taking their lives. It was as simple, and as complicated, as that.

Almost from the day he was born, John Martin Crawford was a troubled individual. Despite the best efforts of a caring and concerned, if somewhat obsessive, mother, John grew from a bullying child into a glue-sniffing, explosive young man. No amount of counselling or psychiatric care, it seems, was able to make a difference to his lifestyle. By the time he was nineteen, Crawford was a killer. Within five years of killing Mary Jane Serloin, he was released on parole. He quickly demonstrated his inability to function in society, and he was returned to prison. But another chance was not far away. He served barely seven years for taking a human life, and that time behind bars did nothing to address his severe emotional and substance-abuse problems. By the late 1980s, it was clear that John Crawford was evolving into a monster, but no one, including his mother and a score of mental health professionals, was able to intervene and prevent the tragedies that were to follow.

Chapter Six

A CASE OF MANSLAUGHTER

Ayo Iihtsipaitapiiyo'pa,
Ayo noohksikimma'tookinnaana Soksiipaitapiisini,
Anakoohka aiyika'kimmaahpinnaana,
Anakoohka aikimmapiiyipitsspinnaana,
Anakoohka aisakaki'tsspinnaana Niipaitapiisini,
Anakoohka ayiistapaotsistapi'takihpinnaana,
Ayo noohksikimma'tookinnaana, amoistsi
nitaatsimoi' ihkaaninnaanistsi,
Anoohka ksiistsikoiihka,
Kamotaana.

Oh Source of Our Life,
Oh grant us the Good Life,
Let us persevere,
Let us be compassionate,
Let us cherish Life,
Let us be more and more understanding,
Oh grant us these, our prayers, on this day,
Let us be safe.

—Peigan prayer

There can be few Canadian cities less prone to violence than Lethbridge, a community of sixty-eight thousand deep in the Bible Belt of southern Alberta. If someone could create an ideal city, Mayor David Carpenter boasts, Lethbridge would be it: "It would be a city young families would choose to call home, and it would be a city that values its senior population. It would be a place where people still care about their neighbours, where volunteering is a way of life."

Mayor Carpenter would get little argument. Lethbridge is a prosperous city, law-abiding and socially conscious. But occasionally, even in the best of cities, things can go violently askew. Such was the case two days before Christmas 1981.

Wednesday, December 23, of that year seemed little different from most days for Mary Jane Serloin. She had a few drinks at the Bridge Inn, something to eat at Jim Poon's Chinese Restaurant, and a few laughs with friends when she returned to the pub later. She was a woman with few commitments. Her family consisted largely of the other regulars who frequented the Bridge Inn—or the Bridge, as it was usually called—a blue-collar bar in what was devolving into Lethbridge's skid row. The beverage room was dark and musty, with the usual chrome tables and worn-out chairs with patched vinyl seats. The jukebox played steadily through most of the day, but the pool table didn't generally come to life until later in the afternoon.

By evening, Mary Jane was in more than usually rough shape. She had been drinking all day, and was in no condition to make rational decisions. At some point she ran into nineteen-year-old John Martin Crawford, who was looking to pick up a woman. He, too, had been drinking at the Bridge, and he had noticed Mary Jane. After a few beers, he felt bold enough to make his pitch. Mary Jane had no objection to letting a man buy her a drink. She enjoyed the companionship, however fleeting. So no one was surprised to see the thirty-five-year-old Serloin and young John Crawford sharing a pitcher of draught. John offered Mary Jane a cigarette, and the two gossiped about people they knew in the bar.

If she thought about it at all, Mary Jane Serloin probably considered herself a survivor. She had been in some of the roughest bars in southern Alberta, places where being Native was definitely not an advantage, and, until now, she'd survived them all.

Early the next morning the nude and battered body of a Native woman was found in an alcove behind the old Number 1 firehall, not far from the Bridge Inn. Littered with soiled blankets and sordid garbage, it was a spot frequented by solvent sniffers and drunks. In the midst of it lay Mary Jane Serloin, her flesh disfigured by bruises and lacerations, and deep bite marks on her neck and breasts. A transient had stumbled upon her corpse, perhaps while going to the alcove to sleep or to relieve himself. There was no snow on the ground, although it was almost Christmas.

News of Mary Jane Serloin's death generated two brief reports; both buried in the second section of the Lethbridge *Herald*, in the two editions following her death. On the Peigan reserve west of Fort Macleod, approximately seventy-five kilometres from Lethbridge, the news was received with more attention. Mary Jane's sister, Justine English, was shattered by it. She knew her sister had been living on the wild side, but she had never thought it would come to this. She wondered if Mary Jane's ex-husband was to blame.

Almost as hard to bear as Mary Jane's death was that no one seemed to care about it. Officials never got in touch with Justine or any other members of the family. There was nothing in the media other than six column inches in the *Herald*, which seems peculiar, especially for a town unaccustomed to this sort of violence.

Even so, police in Lethbridge moved quickly to apprehend the killer. Less than eight hours after Mary Jane's body had been found, officers picked up John Crawford at his parents' home in north Lethbridge. The arrest was uneventful. The young man offered no resistance. Police reports describe Crawford as "very quiet and very subdued."

The quick arrest was the result of "good old-fashioned leg work," according to Bill Plomp, then a detective sergeant working in the identification unit of the Lethbridge police department. Investigators making the rounds of the skid row bars learned that the couple had left the Bridge Inn, less than a block from the old firehall, at about 10:00 PM on Wednesday. No one recalled seeing

Serloin again that night, but Crawford was observed again before midnight when he returned to the bar and drank several more beers. Although only nineteen, Crawford was known to many people who frequented the Bridge Inn, and investigators had little difficulty putting a name to the man who had left with Mary Jane Serloin and then returned alone.

The state of the victim's body told the police they were looking for a special breed of criminal. There were bite marks on her chest, clavicle, cheek, and breasts. There was blood around her mouth, as well as vomit. There was severe bruising of the upper torso, face, and chin, as well as lacerations to the head. At some point, a brick had been slammed into her abdomen, just below the rib cage; a pathologist later found more than a litre of blood in the abdominal cavity caused by the rupturing of the portal vein. Clearly, this was not a simple case of rough sex going too far. Mary Jane Serloin had been overpowered by a much larger, much stronger person who had then turned sadistically and criminally violent.

The investigators took their time processing the crime scene, although it soon became apparent that gathering hair fibres and other specimens would be futile given the number of people who regularly visited the alcove. The evidence of drinking, sleeping, impromptu sex, and various bodily functions occurring behind the abandoned brick firehall was ubiquitous and overwhelming. There was too much evidence of everything to pin down one particular act. In the end, it didn't really matter.

At the police station, Crawford proved to be a co-operative suspect. According to him, the story went like this: "We were making out and she started choking. I pounded on her to stop her from choking. I panicked and ran away." He offered no explanation for the teeth marks and other injuries, beyond suggesting that someone else may have been responsible. It was an account so lame as to insult the intelligence of the investigating officers. They wasted no time in playing their trump card. You can help us prove it wasn't you, they told him, by allowing us to take a mould of your teeth. The teenager readily agreed, and a Lethbridge denturist was called in. The wax impressions removed any lingering doubt in Detective Sergeant Plomp's mind. Crawford had unique teeth; the match to the bite marks was unmistakable.

"I was a fingerprint technician, and had limited knowledge of bite marks," Plomp recalled, "but I knew we had the right guy. He immediately went from being a suspect to being the accused."

Crawford was charged with first-degree murder, for the police believed that he had killed Mary Jane Serloin during a sexual attack, thereby justifying the most serious charge in the Canadian Criminal Code. He made his first court appearance in early January. The case still failed to generate much in the way of media attention, either then or six months later, in mid-June, when Crawford agreed to plead guilty to a reduced charge of manslaughter, thus eliminating the need for an anticipated three-day trial. In that event, it took less than an hour for John Martin Crawford to enter his plea and receive a ten-year sentence—a penalty Art Larson, Crawford's lawyer, described as "pretty healthy" for manslaughter.

Larson, a graduate of the University of Saskatchewan law school, is acknowledged as one of the top defence lawyers in southern Alberta. Well groomed and nattily attired, he moves quickly and speaks rapidly. Sergeant Plomp describes him as "one of Lethbridge's best criminal lawyers."

With Larson in the picture, it was conceivable that the police and prosecutors opted for the best deal they could get, recognizing that a conviction was not guaranteed with such a formidable opponent defending the accused. Since Mary Jane Serloin had, according to the pathologist, literally drowned in her own vomit, a skilled lawyer could raise serious doubts in a jury's mind as to Crawford's intent, despite all the horrific evidence to the contrary. If a jury could be tempted to accept the defence theory that it was Serloin's own alcohol consumption that had led to her death—that the other injuries were, in fact, merely secondary—they could have opted to give Crawford the benefit of the doubt and set him free.

According to prosecutor Jim Langston, now a Queen's Bench justice in Alberta, the Crown accepted the manslaughter plea only after "examining what we had available to us and basing our decision on that evidence." Speaking to sentence, Langston emphasized the seriousness of the injuries inflicted on Mary Jane Serloin, and suggested that she and Crawford had left the bar for a sexual liaison that led to Crawford beating and biting the woman, which, in turn, precipitated her vomiting, and ultimately her death.

In passing sentence, Mr. Justice L. D. MacLean said that one of the most troubling aspects of the attack was Crawford's callous disregard for what had just happened, returning, as he did, to the tavern for beer and pizza minutes after taking the life of Mary Jane Serloin. In his judgement, MacLean conceded that the ten-year sentence could be considered lighter than normal, but insisted that it adequately reflected society's abhorrence to such a crime. Evidently, the judge felt Crawford's relative youth and "deficient cerebral condition" were mitigating factors in sentencing.

When Bill Plomp, now retired from the police force and working as a private investigator in Lethbridge, learned of Crawford's subsequent killing spree in Saskatchewan, it came as no surprise. He had seen no remorse in Crawford, he said, after the death of Mary Jane Serloin.

With Crawford convicted and off to prison, the Lethbridge *Herald* finally gave the murder some play: a twelve-inch report with no byline that outlined the details that had been presented in court the previous day. The story focused on the injuries suffered by the victim, and comments by the lawyers and Mr. Justice MacLean. In the fourth paragraph, Serloin was finally identified as "35-year-old Mary Serloin of Brocket [a town on the Peigan reserve] whose nude body was found in a narrow alcove . . ."

Throughout the entire sequence of events, beginning with the murder at Christmas and the sentencing of John Martin Crawford on June 16, 1982, members of Mary Jane's family were nowhere to be seen. It would have been a simple matter for justice officials to locate Serloin's family and brief them on the case. Similarly, the local media could have shown some interest, even a little compassion for a family that had suffered the loss of a loved one. But when John Martin Crawford appeared in court and entered his plea, there were only a few observers, and Mary Jane Serloin's family was not among them. Their role in seeing that justice was meted out to the man who had taken Mary Jane's life was neither sought nor offered.

"They didn't even have the decency to let me know what was going on," said Justine English. "I really would have wanted to see him, to see what the guy that killed my sister looked like."

It is perhaps not surprising that Justine English harbours a distrust of white society. An intelligent, energetic woman in her mid-fifties, she has seen and experienced enough in her own life to form such an attitude, but it was the death of her younger sister that solidified her conviction that Native people are considered inferior in Canadian society.

The Peigan reserve lies mostly in an immense valley thirty kilometres west of Fort Macleod. It is a tranquil setting. Cattle graze on the gently rolling hills, and sunshine splashes on the prairie grass as far as the eye can see. To an outsider, it looks much like any other reserve community. The town of Brocket, on the reserve, contains a community centre, businesses, and recreation facilities. Away from the townsite, the homes are sited far apart. Most are small and white, containing a kitchen, living room, dining room, and three minuscule bedrooms. Most, too, could benefit from a visit from a battery of skilled trades people. Shoddy workmanship and inferior materials combined with the relentless onslaught of the wind and, in some cases, neglect and abuse, have caused many of the homes to fall into disrepair. If not for the fact that they were located on an Indian reserve, many would long ago have been declared uninhabitable.

The wind, sometimes gentle, more often wild and unpredictable, is something a person never gets used to, Justine English confesses—this from a person whose ancestors have inhabited this same valley for a hundred generations. Justine, the first daughter born to May and Julius English, arrived on May 6, 1942. Four years later, in Brocket, Mary Jane was born. The early years were happy ones for the girls and their parents. Julius English was a man of great warmth, although he could be stern and opinionated, particularly in his role as a band councillor. He served under four chiefs—John Yellow Horn, Peter Smith, Maurice McDougall, and Nelson Small Legs—and when he died on February 22, 1991, the tributes were numerous and sincere. Friends and family remembered a man who had served his country in the Second World War (a country in which he did not have the right to vote in federal elections until 1960) and returned to take his place in the community as an active member of the church, the band council, and numerous sports and cultural organizations.

"Treat a person right and you will be treated the same way," Julius English often said.

The father was a source of pride to his daughters. Years later, sitting at her kitchen table, Justine English produced a black-and-white photograph from her collection of family mementoes and pointed to a smiling Mary Jane sitting in the second row of a class picture. She was tiny for her age, which would have been five or six, and one of only three or four Indian children in the class of twenty-five. Surrounded by her classmates, Mary Jane smiled directly into the camera, a beautiful child who had already known her share of tragedy.

Although it happened half a century ago, Justine described it as though it were yesterday: a team of horses her father was driving suddenly spooked, tipping the buggy in which Mary Jane, Justine, and their mother were riding. May English, the most seriously hurt, was rushed to hospital in Edmonton. There it was discovered that she had tuberculosis.

"The day of the accident was the last time I saw her," Justine said in a small, distant voice. "She came back in a box."

Shortly after her mother's death, Mary Jane went to live with relatives elsewhere on the reserve. Justine recalled the day they took the baby from her father's arms: "A car came and picked her up and took her away. That was it; she was gone. For a while, I forgot I even had a sister."

Occasionally Mary Jane was brought to visit Justine and her father, or Justine would visit her sister in her new home, and the girls would renew their sisterhood by wrestling and chasing each other about the house. Justine loved to pull Mary Jane around the yard in a wagon, stopping occasionally to slip into the house and steal cookies for her little sister.

Behind the infrequent but joyous family reunions there lurked yet another family tragedy, although Justine did not learn of it until after Mary Jane's death in 1981. It was only then that the elder sister discovered that Mary Jane had been sexually abused by a male relative and that his wife, if she had not actually participated in the abuse, at least condoned it.

"Mary Jane and I were never left alone," Justine remembered. "I think they were afraid Mary Jane would tell me something." No one dared say anything while it was happening; the secret was safe within the family. "It really hurts me. I get angry at my own relatives. They all knew. But there's nothing I could do now."

If Mary Jane's childhood was traumatic, her transition to adulthood was equally grim. In her early twenties she married Norman Serloin, a much older white man. They had one son, Troy, born in 1972. It was not a happy marriage. Norman and Mary Jane drank and fought constantly, and they were forever moving from one small town to another in hopes that Norman could get work. Justine recalled once visiting them in Magrath, a town of thirteen hundred south of Lethbridge. Norman was working as a labourer on a nearby farm. Norman was always on his best behaviour when Justine was visiting, "acting like the best brother-in-law," but the elder sister saw beyond his words and behaviour. Mary Jane never complained to her, but Justine suspected that Mary Jane would be in trouble after the visit if she did complain.

When the marriage eventually dissolved—Norman and Mary Jane split for good sometime in 1979 or 1980—Justine's little sister learned quickly that temporary happiness, at least, could be found in the bar. By then a short, chubby woman with dark eyes and raven black hair, Mary Jane quickly gained a reputation for being easygoing and fun.

"She had a few friends," Justine observed, "but her only entertainment was the bar. There were a lot of old men in the bar who knew her. She didn't go to bed with them, but they looked after her. I don't blame Mary Jane for the life she led. She didn't know any better. Nobody ever showed her anything else. She considered what she was doing normal."

The death of Mary Jane Serloin in 1981 changed the life of Justine English forever. She still calls it murder, refusing to accept that a brutal killing can be reduced to an act of manslaughter, even semantically. She states the obvious with natural eloquence: "We're people too. We have feelings. Why are we so degraded by the system?"

A mug shot of John Crawford taken by the Saskatoon city police in 1992 is her first sight of the man who killed her sister. Justine shakes her head. He has no conscience, she says. "I would like to see him under the ground, too, but that's not going to solve anything."

Would it have solved anything if John Crawford had been convicted of at least second-degree murder in 1982? Would he then have been in a position to take the lives of at least three more women a decade later? Second-degree carries a life sentence with no possibility of parole for ten years. It is conceivable, considering Mr. Justice MacLean's remarks about Crawford's callous disregard for the act he had just committed, that a judge might have sentenced him to a much longer term before he was eligible for parole. A stiffer sentence could well have seen John Martin Crawford behind bars well into the 1990s. A life sentence would have further subjected him to the conscientious attentions of a parole officer. Any hint of violence would have landed him back in prison immediately and indefinitely. But on June 15, 1992, John Martin Crawford's sentence came to an end.

By then, it was already too late.

Chapter Seven

In Pursuit of His Prey

"Do her, Bill, or I'll punch the shit out of her."
—John Martin Crawford

For almost four months in 1994 an RCMP surveillance team watched John Martin Crawford on a nightly basis, following his every move once he left his mother's home at 113 Avenue Q North. The home, which accommodates a dozen men with varying degrees of physical and psychological needs, is located in the first block north of 22nd Street, a main thoroughfare that runs from the extreme west end of the city into the downtown area. The house is a block away from the busy intersection of Avenue P and 22nd Street, which boasts, among other things, a Shell gas bar and car wash, a 7-Eleven convenience store, a Rogers Video outlet, Robin's Donuts, and a small strip mall that had once included an adult video store. On that stretch of 22nd, there is a smattering of older, mostly dilapidated homes, generally occupied by families subsisting on welfare.

Stretching five blocks to the west, from Avenue P to Avenue U, a hodgepodge of three-floor walk-ups, built in the 1960s and '70s, dominates the street. Some are well-maintained and bear such romantic, if wildly inappropriate, names as "Camelot" and "Lancelot." Others are clearly ageing cash cows, maintained at the bare minimum by their landlords. From the outside, many of these three-storey slums look more like fortresses than homes. Heavy wire mesh covers the lower windows in a crude attempt to keep unwanted visitors from entering the suites. It's a futile strategy, since few of the buildings have operating security systems, or even doors that lock properly.

Inside these blocks, it's a rare door that doesn't show some signs of forced entry. The tenants, mostly Native and mostly welfare recipients, occupy apartments that bespeak the transgressions of previous tenants. The walls are battered and often stained with spattered blood indicative of previous violence or drug abuse. Windows are invariably cracked. Screens, where they exist, are torn and filthy. The landlords collect regular and generally inflated rents from provincial Social Services and always manage to keep half a step ahead of the building inspectors by performing only the most essential repairs. The tenants seldom complain. Most are grateful simply to have a roof over their head. Many have nowhere else to turn; their lifestyle has relegated them to Third World living conditions. For some, however, it's no worse than the environment they left or have come to accept as normal on Indian reserves across the country.

South of the busy 22nd Street residential strip, long-time residents of the no-longer aptly named neighbourhood of Pleasant Hill struggle to understand what has happened to their community. Discarded syringes and condoms turn up on lawns, sidewalks, school grounds. Wide-eyed girls, some as young as ten, mimic the body language of their older sisters, hoping to catch the eyes of johns who cruise the streets. It's a violent world, in which drug trafficking and prostitution play a dominant role.

This was John Martin Crawford's playground. From the time he was released from the Prince Albert Penitentiary in March 1989 after serving time for manslaughter in the death of Mary Jane

Serloin until he was arrested for murder in mid-January 1995, Crawford cruised this neighbourhood relentlessly, his pattern only interrupted by periodic incarcerations.

The officers who tailed him in various nondescript pickup trucks and unmarked cars quickly learned that Crawford was a creature of habit. On a typical evening during those four months, he would eat dinner at home, then jump into Victoria Crawford's sporty Cougar and drive down to Avenue N to pick up one of his few friends, Jimmy Mason. The next stop was invariably Tim Horton's on 22nd Street and Avenue D. John would saunter through the door, turn left into the seating area, and park himself—always at the same table near a window—with Jimmy a step behind. One night, a member of the surveillance team arrived at the donut shop before John and Jimmy made their appearance. The officer purposely took John's favourite seat. When Crawford walked in moments later, he stopped in his tracks and stared in confusion, then led Jimmy to the next table.

Once they had downed a cup of coffee and a refill each, the two men would begin their rounds—or rather, John's rounds, for Jimmy was not always with him. The route rarely varied. John would head west on 22nd Street, make a left turn at Avenue P and another at 21st Street. Prostitutes worked 21st between Avenue K and Avenue W, standing on corners or sitting on the steps of apartment blocks. John would slow down, searching for familiar faces, commenting on physical attributes and asking prices. He knew many of the prostitutes along the stroll, and he knew better than to approach a white girl. The Saskatoon Police Service operates frequent sting operations to pick up johns, but Native girls were almost certainly not undercover cops. John had been convicted of trying to pick up an undercover cop in December 1990 and fined $250. He wouldn't make that mistake again. The Native women were far less trouble.

If there was nothing to grab his attention on 21st Street he would turn right at Avenue M and stop at the corner, checking out the sidewalk in front of the Museum of Ukrainian Culture. Further down the block, prostitutes could often be found lingering in front of St. George's Ukrainian Catholic Cathedral. If not,

John knew there would usually be hookers sitting on the steps of the Parish Hall at the corner of 20th Street and Avenue M.

If nothing stopped him here, it was down 20th Street, where the occasional prostitute might be found looking for business between Avenue M and Avenue B. Although 20th was no longer a preferred location for working girls, there were often one or two women at the corner of Avenue I and 20th, a block from the "Booze Can." At Avenue B, John would occasionally turn left and drive alongside the Albany, turning into the lane behind the old hotel. There weren't often working girls outside the bar, but it was sometimes a good place to find a woman who had just left the beverage room and might be enticed into the car. On most nights, though, he pulled into the curb lane and turned right. He'd survey the action outside the Barry Hotel—there was always *something* going on—then continue on to 19th Street and turn right again.

The next few blocks offered a good chance of meeting a prostitute, so he drove slowly until he reached Avenue J South. There he would turn right again, toward 20th Street, and creep up the narrow residential avenue, his view obstructed by parked cars. One night, with his watchers a safe distance behind, he drove into the back of another car while checking out a woman on the sidewalk. He was going so slowly that there was little damage to either vehicle. Back on to 20th, he returned to his primary area, the Pleasant Hill stroll along 21st Street. He could cover the whole route in no more than fifteen or twenty minutes, depending on how many stops he made along the way.

John made this same circuit as many as fourteen or fifteen times an evening, virtually every day. Rarely did the pattern vary. By the winter of 1994, Victoria Crawford had placed her son on a strict curfew, and he was usually home around 9:00 PM. This was in stark contrast to the period between 1990 and 1992 when John roamed at will, often spending the entire night cruising the streets. Victoria had tightened the leash after John was accused of raping Janet Sylvestre in 1992. The courts had tightened it further by sending him to the Saskatoon Correctional Centre for most of 1993 after he brutally assaulted a young man.

But whether it was 1992 or 1994, whether he was under curfew or not, his interests never varied. He had no interest in sports, in making friends outside his meagre circle of like-minded cronies, or in seeing other parts of the city. Round and round he drove, looking for sex.

Defying the odds, since he was known as a bad trick on the stroll, Crawford managed to pick up three or four women a week. He paid them with money his mother gave him for helping around the home. Generally, it was quick and uneventful. One Saskatoon prostitute, known as "Spin," claims to have sold her services to John at least twice with no problems. He paid what the Native woman asked, offered no violence, and delivered her back to 21st Street immediately after their business was concluded. When Crawford was arrested in 1995, Spin was surprised to hear that he had been charged with three murders. Her dealings with him had always been positive, or as positive as such dealings can ever be.

Other women were not so fortunate. In the spring of 1992 Louise Alice LeMay, then twenty-three years old, was new to the business and not particularly comfortable in her role. She preferred to work the stroll in the afternoons, servicing ten to fifteen men a week, rarely staying out beyond 9:00 PM. It was safer that way, she reasoned, although she once came within an inch of losing her life.

In January 1995, after Crawford's arrest, Louise went to the police with an interesting, if appalling, story. Investigators knew that getting the young woman before a jury would be next to impossible, as judges rarely allowed similar-fact evidence to be heard in court. (Similar-fact evidence provides details of actions on the part of the accused that the Crown hopes will establish a predilection for a certain type of activity.) Just the same, they thought, her story might offer compelling insights into Crawford's behaviour when he was in a mindless rage. Eva Taysup, Shelley Napope, and Calinda Waterhen were dead. The horrors they had suffered at the hands of their killer would never be truly known. Louise LeMay could at least offer a glimpse of what Crawford was capable of.

In the spring of 1992, Louise agreed to provide oral sex to two men for a fee of $140. The men, who turned out to be John Martin Crawford and Bill Corrigan, could not possibly have afforded her services at that rate, and likely had no intention of paying. That would place LeMay in an extremely vulnerable position. But she didn't know that as she got into the old green Nova that Victoria Crawford owned at the time. They headed south along Avenue P, then turned at Garfield Street, a block-long industrial alley running behind Vern's Car Wash at 11th Street. It was one of John's favourite places to take prostitutes. A concrete manufacturer used an unkempt lot behind the car wash to store surplus and sub-standard inventory. Septic tanks, culverts, and concrete stairways share ground space with gangly weeds and the assorted garbage of urban industrial decay. Three rutted, potholed paths cut through the lot to points of privacy where someone who did not want to be seen could avoid unwanted company. One can only imagine what was going through the young prostitute's mind as John pulled into the lot and stopped.

According to the usual pattern, Bill Corrigan got out of the car and let John get down to business. Bill lit a cigarette and wandered over to the car wash.

"Get in the back seat," Crawford told the prostitute, and she did as she was told.

"Lock the doors and take your clothes off," he added as he unzipped his jeans.

"What for?" Louise wanted to know. She had agreed to oral sex, nothing more. "I'm not doing a lay," she reminded him.

Immediately enraged, Crawford put his hands around the young woman's neck and began to squeeze. Louise struggled, but she was no match for the much-larger man. She lost consciousness. By the time she came to, John had removed her top and was in the process of lifting up her bra. Terrified, she took off the rest of her clothes and submitted to him, reasoning that it was better to give in than to die. But Crawford continued to choke her even as he penetrated her, causing her to black out several more times. When the attack was over, Crawford allowed her to get out of the car. But he wasn't finished with her yet.

"You do her, Bill," he said when Corrigan returned from his stroll. "Get in the back seat with her."

Corrigan, never a man of great courage, did as he was told. But he was scared, Louise told the police: "I could tell in his voice." Fear and sex make bad companions, but Corrigan didn't want Crawford to know that he had been unable to perform. As he had done on other occasions, he exposed himself, and LeMay simulated oral sex for several minutes. Crawford wasn't fooled.

"Do her, Bill," he warned, "or I'll punch the shit out of her."

But quite evidently Corrigan couldn't "do her," and he soon gave up and got out of the back seat.

"Come on, Johnny, I can't come," he said, as Louise struggled to put on her clothes. "Let's get out of here."

Crawford fell silent, and for a moment the young woman thought that might be the end of it. With everyone back in the car and the car moving again, she thought he might be taking her back to 20th Street. He wasn't. He headed out on 11th Street, beyond the city limits and into the country. Something of his rage translated to his driving as he sped along Valley Road, past the Saskatoon Berry Barn and the Moon Lake golf course. Then he turned off the pavement onto gravel, and a few minutes later pulled into a field alongside a grove of willows.

The two men got out of the car. Crawford opened the trunk and pulled out a bottle of wine as well as a quantity of wieners and potato chips while Corrigan headed for the bushes. He had to relieve himself, he said. He did not see John or Louise again that night, which turned out to be a long one. The weather was foul, cold and raining, and Corrigan ended up walking the entire sixteen kilometres back to the city, cursing his friend every step of the way.

Crawford's mood, Louise was relieved to see as she watched him taking great gulps of the wine, had improved as dramatically and inexplicably as it had first gone sour. Whether he had arrived with the intention to commit murder, have a picnic, or simply drink wine, it is impossible to say, but Louise was only too happy to agree when he suggested that they head back. He started the

Nova and popped it into gear, departing without a thought for Bill Corrigan.

Crawford stopped on 11th Street near the cement factory. He offered Louise the wieners and potato chips—a belated act of chivalry?—then asked, "You going to call the cops?"

Her response probably saved her life. "No, I've got warrants out," she said truthfully.

Evidently pleased with her answer, John offered no objection when she told him she needed to get to a washroom. She ran from the Nova and into the littered lot behind the car wash, where she concealed herself in a large concrete pipe, in the dark, out of the rain and safely away from John Crawford. It was the last she saw of him until his face appeared on the front page of the Saskatoon *StarPhoenix* in January 1995. Only then did she realize how close she had come to dying that night.

Melanie Fiddler had a similarly close call with John Martin Crawford in the summer of 1992. Then twenty-two years old, she was returning from a house party on Avenue I early one morning. She was extremely drunk, but had managed to walk ten blocks—two steps forward, one step back—when she heard a car turning onto Avenue S South behind her. Her feet were sore, she had no money for a cab, and she was a long way from her home in Massey Place, a working-class neighbourhood on the western fringe of the city. Thrusting her thumb out, she didn't bother to look up until she heard the car slow down and stop. It was an ugly, green, four-door sedan.

"Get in."

Melanie got in, grateful to be off her feet and convinced that she would be crawling into her own bed in a few minutes. But John Crawford had other ideas. It was 5:00 AM and he had been driving around most of the night. He had pretty much abandoned hope of finding a woman. By this time of the morning, John knew his chances were slim. But he'd decided to take one more tour through Pleasant Hill. His mother wouldn't be up for another hour, and if he could slip in quietly and make his way to his basement bedroom, she would never know what time he had come in.

So he was driving down 21st Street behind St. Paul's Hospital, checking out the avenues on both sides as he passed. He spotted a solitary figure on Avenue S—a woman, alone, obviously drunk. He probably could hardly believe his luck when she stuck out her thumb. That made everything easier. Seconds later Melanie Fiddler was being driven south out of the city, to a place she had never seen before.

John stopped the car in a secluded spot behind a row of bushes within sight of the river. There was no conversation. He simply pounced on the terrified woman. He grabbed her by the hair and started choking her, then forced her into the back seat, where he strangled her until she passed out. She was naked when she regained consciousness, at which point, she said, "He pulled down his joggers and raped me."

It took only a few minutes, then it was over. Melanie grabbed her clothes and went to the river, where she drank deeply, without thought for the safety or cleanliness of the water. Crawford, too, was thirsty, and followed suit, cupping his large hands and drawing water from the South Saskatchewan River to his thick lips. Then, without a word, he returned to his car and sped away. Melanie was left to fend for herself. She walked for what seemed an eternity before coming to a yard, where an obliging farmer drove her back to the city. She told him not to say anything to the police.

Finally home, the young woman tearfully told her mother that a heavy white man had raped her. He had almost choked her to death, she said. She had never been so frightened in her life. But she begged her mother not to go to the police.

"I was too scared," she explained.

She still is, even with John Martin Crawford behind bars.

Melanie Fiddler is not her real name.

Chapter Eight

A MISSING DAUGHTER

"Mom, I miss you a lot. It is hard for me not seeing you everyday and waking me up for school and you giving me shit if I don't come home. Mom, are you going to let me come and live with you? I don't want to be anywhere else but with my family."

—Shelley Napope
May 9, 1990

Hubert and Merle Napope are the first to acknowledge that they made mistakes in raising their three children. They drank too much. They left the kids alone to fend for themselves too often. They understand now that the Department of Social Services acted appropriately when the children were apprehended and sent to foster homes, sometimes for weeks at a time. But in the early 1980s an event occurred over which they had no control. It changed the Napopes' lives forever and, Hubert and Merle firmly believe, eventually led to the death of their youngest daughter at the hands of John Martin Crawford.

Hubert Napope and Merle Baldhead have been together since the early seventies. When their first daughter was born, they lived on the One Arrow Reserve east of Duck Lake, not far from the Beardy's and Okemasis First Nation where both Hubert and Merle had family connections. The couple was very young and not yet ready to care for a baby. It was decided that Charlotte would be better off living with Merle's mother. But by the time Shelley arrived on July 31, 1976, things were looking up, and Hubert and Merle were content in their small home.

"It was a good life on the reserve," Merle remembers. "We had everything we needed." And when Shelley arrived it brought Merle and Hubert closer. The baby was a joy from the time they brought her home from the hospital in nearby Rosthern. She grew into a happy, inquisitive youngster, quick to make friends with children and adults alike. "She wasn't ever shy," according to her mother. "She would come up to you and ask, 'Who are you?' People used to love her because she wasn't shy."

A year after Shelley arrived, Hubert Jr. was born, and Shelley delighted in playing with her little brother as they grew up together. Shelley and Hubert Jr.—she called him Huey—remained close throughout their childhood. Big sister often played a protective role, particularly when she reached the age of twelve and towered over Huey, who was developing at a more modest pace. Later, it was Huey who played the role of protector.

Hubert augmented the family income by working as a fine-option agent on the reserve, arranging work for people who had been convicted of misdemeanours and had opted to work off the fine rather than pay cash. Hubert believes that he was targeted for an act of retribution. The summer that he and Merle and the two kids went to Vauxhall, Alberta, where Hubert picked sugar beets for a month, they returned to One

Arrow to a scene of utter, mindless destruction. Their house was in shambles. The windows were broken. The doors were knocked off their hinges. There were holes in every wall. The cupboards had been emptied. Food and dishes were strewn throughout the house.

Merle and Hubert were devastated and heartbroken, not just at the destruction of their home, but by the fact that someone had hated them so much that they would do something like that. They went to the chief, who told them they would have to demolish the house. There wasn't anything worth saving.

"But don't worry," the chief assured them, "we'll build you a new house next year."

Next year never arrived. Despite pleas to the Department of Indian Affairs, members of the Saskatchewan Legislature, and even the media, there would be no new home for the Napope family on One Arrow. Eventually Merle and Hubert decided that their only alternative was to move to Saskatoon, where housing was more abundant. The family could start over there, and Shelley and Huey could find a good school.

In January 1984, Shelley was enrolled at St. Michael School on 33rd Street, not far from the family's rental home on Idylwyld Drive. Outgoing and restless, the seven-year-old excelled in music, art, and physical education, her favourite subjects. Her teacher, Mrs. Stolar, praised her efforts and enthusiasm in these areas, but noted that Shelley would need to put some additional effort into language and mathematics if she were to succeed in grade two. Her attendance was average; she missed only eight days in the six months she attended St. Michael.

As Shelley grew, though, Merle and Hubert began to see signs that not all was right in their little girl's world. She was skipping school, and occasionally causing problems in class. The principal often called. Shelley didn't like being told what to do, he said, and she resented the authority figures at the school. Shelley's parents knew they had to share at least some of the blame for their daughter's erratic and disrespectful behaviour.

"We drank quite a bit," Hubert now admits. "To tell you we didn't would be a lie."

The solution, the family decided, would be to send Shelley to St. Michael's Residential School in Duck Lake, eighty kilometres north of Saskatoon. In the more disciplined and supervised environment, they hoped, Shelley's rebellious streak might become more manageable.

St. Michael's was once a residential school operated by the Catholic Church, but by the time Shelley attended the Saskatoon Tribal Council ran the school. There, Shelley blossomed once again in her favourite subjects. "You sing really well," her grade four teacher wrote on her third-term report card. "You are fun in Phys. Ed. and you can do good art work when you take your time." As for spelling, mathematics, and science, Ms. Cameron could only offer encouragement: "Don't give up, keep trying, I know you can do it."

But Shelley needed more than encouragement. She didn't like taking orders, she didn't like living in the residence. Hubert and Merle tried to visit her on as many weekends as possible, but Shelley ran away numerous times, frightening her parents and frustrating the social workers who had to track her down. Once she went missing for four days.

Summer was Shelley's season. She loved slamming the classroom door and knowing she didn't have to go to school again for a long time. She and Huey went to Bible Camp. They spent whole days at the swimming pool, or picking berries in the countryside around Duck Lake. They were active, happy children when Shelley didn't have to go to school. But it can't be summer all the time, and Shelley dreaded the day she would have to return to St. Michael's. Grades six and seven were among the most chaotic years of Shelley's life. She ran away constantly, hitching rides into Saskatoon and disappearing into the street life there, where she made new friends, most of whom were older and wiser to the ways of the street. She was growing up far too quickly.

Hubert, no stranger to the hazards and pitfalls of street life, tried to reason with her. But his warnings and experience had no more effect on Shelley than they would have on any high-spirited teenager with a growing addiction to excitement.

Her mother remembers how she would stay over at a friend's for the night, and it would turn into two or three days, then: "I'd see her and her eyes would be glassy, and she would smell like glue."

Merle knew Shelley was sniffing solvents and using drugs, but she was powerless to control it. When Shelley was at home with the family, she would often retreat to her room in the basement. There she would crank up the volume on her stereo enough that Merle and Hubert couldn't hear her prying open the window and crawling out. The police were called so many times that after a while they didn't bother looking for her, the Napopes believe. "They'd say, 'Oh, Shelley again.' I know they were getting tired of it."

When Shelley was fourteen, she became a ward of Social Services. The department started placing her in foster homes. Not surprisingly, living with strangers, she rebelled and ran back to her street friends. It was around that time that she began coming to the attention of the police as something more than a missing child. Her offences included breaking and entering as well as other, less serious charges, including numerous failures to appear in court. She regularly ended up in Kilburn Hall, a facility for young offenders in Saskatoon, and once for a short time in the Paul Dojack, a similar facility in Regina.

Letters she wrote from these facilities in 1990 and 1991 reveal much about the personality and mental state of Shelley Napope during this period. She is, by turns, remorseful, teasing, and playfully sarcastic. Occasionally, she displays anger toward her family. She is clearly frustrated and lonely, anxious to return to the arms of her mother, whom she fears has abandoned her.

Visually, the letters defy explanation. Perhaps a handwriting expert might begin to interpret the significance of the varied penmanship, but to any other person it would appear as if the letters had been written by several different people. Shelley usually wrote on foolscap. Some of her letters are neatly printed in pen or pencil and fill both sides of the page. One, to brother Huey, whom she had taken to calling "Mister Brown," was only seven lines long. Sometimes the writing is minuscule and crabbed; other times the letters are formed with bold, dramatic sweeps that leave room for only five or six words on a line. The spelling is eccentric, to say the least, and the language is that of a child who has clearly not applied herself to the rules of grammar. Even so, the emotions she experiences while incarcerated are as palpable as they are heart-wrenching.

She began every letter with "Hi!"

In a May 1991 letter to her mother, she wrote: "So how is the Birthday girl doing today. Me not bad I guess it could be better." She went on to describe her feelings of loneliness and regret, urging Merle to phone or come for a visit: "I am crying right now because I miss you very much and it hurts me to see you hurt. I care for you a lot and I would do anything even if you get hurt I will hurt myself real bad just for you."

On the same day, she wrote a letter to her brother, and decorated it with peel-and-stick cartoon characters:

> Dear Huey,
>
> Hi there bro! So are you going to ask mom to come and visit me because all the other girls moms and dads come and visit them and bring them chips and pop but not mom and dad. Huey, when you were at school I told Mom and Dad to come and visit me here and they said they would but they lied to me and I was waiting for them.
>
> Huey, I want to come home but I don't know if Mom will let me. I think Mom is still mad at me for leaving home. It is hard for me in here. I wish someone would come visit me. Huey I miss you very much and I wish I never left home. I would be having fun with you right now. Huey are you mad at me for leaving home. Huey draw me a few of your pictures and mail them to me. You are a good drawer.
>
> Keep on smiling my one and only brother.
> Love your sister Shelley Gail Napope

One letter, undated but likely written in the summer of 1991, opens: "Hi there! It's me Shelley, remember." In large, clear printing, Shelley discusses the fact that she has become a ward of the court and will soon be turned over to a couple named Gwen and Gunnar: "I told you they were going to take me away from the family, they did. I am still your daughter and everything but I am the ward. You know what that means."

In another letter, after wishing her parents well on their upcoming trek to Alberta to pick sugar beets, Shelley displays a rare level of both maturity and optimism:

> I hope I can come home soon because I miss Huey and Dad because you are my only true family that care about me. Well Mom I am going to go straight and make my life much better. I am going off the street life and go back to school and get good grades and do better. I know I can too, but I never tried to do it. Well that's all I have to say. But I love you always.
>
> Love your daughter
Shelley Gail Napope

The theme is repeated in a rambling missive to her brother, composed around the same time. Her affection for Huey is unmistakable. It allows her to communicate with him on a level where she feels most comfortable:

> Huey Napope
> Hi there bro! So how are you doing? Me just fine. So you passed your grade. That's good for you. At least you are going for your Grade 12 in school. Huey, don't drop out of school because you will not know nothing if you do.
> So what are you going to give me for my birthday. I hope something nice. Just jokes. At least it is from you my one and only brother that I love.

Huey, bro, I am going to tell you this. I am going to straighten out my life. I am going back to school next year and get good grades and then get a good job. One thing that I want from you Huey is not to hate me because I love you and that's true because you are my one and only brother.

I wish never to get myself into any trouble and I wish I was at home.

So who is your new girlfriend? I hope I don't know her. Just joke (Ha-ha) Me, my boyfriend's name is Leslie Roy Bird. We have been going out for seven months and he is nice. He never hits me at all.

Love your one and only sister
Shelley Gail Napope
loves Leslie Roy Bird

Shelley's musings of a calmer, safer life were more than the hollow promises of a young convict, scared and lonely, separated from a family she feared was becoming more distant with each passing day. "She had good dreams," her mother recalls. "She used to tell her brother, 'We won't always be poor. We'll be rich some day, you, me, and Mom and Dad. I'm going to get a good job.'" She spoke of becoming a social worker, or a cop. But somewhere along the way, Merle realized that her daughter's dreams had been shelved as Shelley's restless spirit took over: "She wanted to be her own boss. She hated to be bossed around."

In July 1992, a few days shy of Shelley's sixteenth birthday, Merle and Hubert were preparing for another trip to Alberta. The couple had stopped at the OK Economy on 20th Street so Merle could pick up a few last-minute items. Hubert waited outside, watching the pedestrians on the street. Suddenly he saw Shelley walking with a girlfriend. He called her over just as Merle emerged from the store. The couple told their daughter what they were planning, and asked her to come along.

Shelley, glassy-eyed and smelling of marijuana, agreed readily enough, and got into the van.

Her girlfriend had other ideas. "Our boyfriends are waiting for us," she reminded Shelley, and Shelley changed her mind. Hubert and Merle cajoled and argued and persuaded, but to no avail. Shelley went with her girlfriend instead.

It was the last time they ever saw her.

It wasn't long after they returned from Alberta that Hubert and Merle began to worry about their daughter. She hadn't been around to the house. Nobody had seen her. As they had done countless times before, the Napopes reported her missing to the Saskatoon Police Service. This time the response was different. Shelley was over sixteen now, they said. There wasn't anything they could do.

Stories surfaced occasionally throughout the fall. One had it that Shelley was "living with some white guy near Saskatoon." Another had it that Shelley had been seen in the mall, with a baby. Most people concluded that she had simply disappeared into the downtown street scene, living with friends who shared her desire to be free of the strictures of everyday society.

John Crawford remembers it was late September of 1992 when he murdered Shelley Napope, a girl he thought was named Angie. Her body would not be found for another two years. During that time, Merle and Hubert Napope agonized over their missing daughter, hoping for the best but fearing the worst. Despite their appeals to the police, nothing was done to find Shelley. The police issued no missing person reports, and so the media were unaware of the girl's disappearance.

Merle hadn't seen or heard from Shelley since she and Hubert had left for Alberta in July, but she still bought presents for her and placed them under the tree that Christmas of 1992. It was another two years before her worst fears would be confirmed.

By December 14, 1994, the family had moved to a trailer on the outskirts of Duck Lake, the town where Shelley had once attended residential school. It was a bright, sunny winter day when a RCMP officer from the Rosthern detachment knocked on the door. When he politely removed his cap, Merle knew what he had come to tell her. She burst into tears.

The Napopes had heard about the three sets of skeletal remains that had been uncovered south of Saskatoon in early October. Hubert had had a hunch that one of the unidentified women might be Shelley, but Merle tried to remain positive.

"I hope the Good Spirit is with me to help me find who did this so I can put my daughter to rest," Merle said after learning that Shelley had been positively identified through dental records. "My daughter didn't deserve to die this way."

The next day a mass was held in the community hall on the Beardy's and Okemasis Reserve. More than one hundred friends and family members wept as Mary Cameron, an Elder, delivered a ten-minute homily. "As parents and grandparents," she said, speaking in Cree, "when the children are away from home, all we can do is pray for them."

Ten months later, Mark Brayford informed Crown prosecutor Terry Hinz that the identity of the bodies, including Shelley Napope, would not be an issue at the forthcoming trial of his client, John Martin Crawford. It was that admission that enabled the police to release Shelley's remains to her family. She was buried on the Beardy's and Okemasis Reserve. In her casket, Merle placed the Christmas presents she had wrapped for her missing daughter in 1992.

At the scene of the murder, in a clearing cut out of the dense bush, Merle's father, Eddy Baldhead, a respected Elder, presided over a ceremony to put Shelley Gail Napope's soul to rest. A traditional Indian feast was shared. Ribbons and cloth were hung from the trees. The fragrance of sweet grass wafted throughout the grove. Offerings were burned and left on the ground where Shelley's body had lain for two years.

"When we were at that place," Merle said, "I could hear her calling us . . . When we left I could not look back."

Eight years after Shelley vanished, Merle Napope's anguish has not abated. Every summer, on Shelley's birthday, usually accompanied by an Elder, she visits the gravesite. She needs to remind herself that Shelley is gone: "Sometimes I think that she'll come home, ring the bell, and come through the door."

It is easy to dismiss Shelley Napope as a street kid, a girl who survived by her wits on the very edge of the law, occasionally running afoul of it. It is easy to think of her as a girl who took too many chances and ended up as the victim of a sexual predator. But Shelley was also the precious daughter, the girl with the huge dark eyes that evoked the nickname "Owl" from her grandmother, the girl who never forgot a birthday, the girl who made cards for the family on special occasions, the loving daughter, granddaughter, and sister, who had dreams of living a better life. Who is responsible for the fact that she never lived to realize those dreams?

Chapter Nine

DANCING LEAVES WOMAN

*"I thought she was going to go somewhere
and do something better."*

—Evelyn Martel

Amber Waterhen is an energetic eight-year-old with dancing brown eyes. Everything is right in her world. She has a comfortable home that she shares with her grandparents and a rambunctious collection of cousins and other young relatives. Amber's home, surrounded by a forest of birch trees and overlooking a meandering stream, is fifteen kilometres from Loon Lake, a small resort community on the western edge of central Saskatchewan. The townsite was carved out of what is now the Makwa Sahgaiehean First Nation. It is a four-hour drive from Saskatoon. In Amber's world there is laughter, teasing, and the loving arms of her family. She knows nothing of that other world—the one that stole her mother and her maternal grandmother.

Amber Waterhen is Calinda Waterhen's daughter and,

according to Steve Morningchild, "the spitting image of her mom." Stretching two huge scarred arms out to embrace his granddaughter, Morningchild says, "Calinda was rebellious, headstrong. This one here, she's just like her." The little girl smiles at her grandfather, slips from his grasp, and jumps onto a sofa on the other side of the living room.

Calinda Waterhen was in the Pine Grove correctional facility for women, a provincial institution near Prince Albert, when Amber was born on October 11, 1991. When Calinda was released the following month, she and the baby stayed briefly with her father and stepmother, Georgina Lonechild, Steve Morningchild's second wife.

Calinda came out of Pine Grove in poor shape psychologically, according to her father. Some of the inmates had been fooling around with a Ouija board, which some people regard as an innocent game and others see as a dangerous medium for communicating with the spirit world. Calinda had participated, and her father believes that she "contacted a spirit while she was in there, and when she came out, whatever it was came with her. She used to sit in a chair and then all of a sudden she would jump up and scream. One time she punched a hole in the wall."

A few days later—less than a week after she was released from prison—a troubled Calinda left her baby in the capable hands of Steve and Georgina and headed to Saskatoon. Her family never saw her again.

Steve Morningchild—*Wahpunawasis* in Cree—is a self-educated man, much of it as a result of the time he himself spent in jail. While incarcerated he became a voracious reader, devouring Western fiction and later history books, particularly material dealing with the numbered treaties the Crown entered into with First Nations in the late 1800s. He continues to study the treaties and collects newspaper clippings and other documents, cramming them into a battered old suitcase where they can be quickly produced to support his arguments. Steve has become something of a rebel in First Nations circles, denouncing the Federation of

Saskatchewan Indian Nations (FSIN), the Assembly of First Nations, and the local Meadow Lake Tribal Council. All these organizations have sold Indian people down the river, he alleges. In his own life, he has seen the land promised to his grandfather turned, instead, into the town of Loon Lake. What should have been his rightful inheritance was lost, and his family has suffered as a result.

His life has been a two-part story: the alcoholic years, and the rest. He has pleasant memories of the time he spent working with his grandfather on the trapline near Waterhen Lake, north of Dorintosh, Saskatchewan. Every year, around the middle of March, he would accompany his grandfather to set up a tent, and together they would spend hours in the bush, tending to the trapline. Grandfather was a chief of the Makwa Sahgaiehean people, a position of honour that Steve would eventually have inherited in the days before Indian bands began holding elections for chief and council.

Steve started drinking at the age of thirteen, the same time he quit school and started working on farms in the area. In 1969 he met Margaret Waterhen, who lived in nearby Ministikwan. A year later, Calinda was born.

"I took some tobacco to my grandfather," Morningchild explains. "I told him I wanted my daughter to have a Cree name. He told me her name should be *Nemihkeepakow squewe*. It means 'Dancing Leaves Woman.'" More often, the baby was called Calinda, a name inspired by the Western novels Steve had read in jail.

The birth of Calinda was a brief moment of happiness for Steve and Margaret. But those were tumultuous days for the young couple. Steve was eighteen, Margaret a year younger. He wasn't ready to raise a family, and he also brought some serious personal problems into the relationship with Margaret.

"I was a wife-beater," he admits frankly. "I had seen it in my family, and I figured it was the way everyone acted. I didn't know any better. I was in and out of jail. I did some things I'm not proud of."

The couple separated often; sometimes Steve was in jail, other times he would be roaming around the province. When they were together, they invariably lived with relatives, never enjoying the luxury of having a home of their own. In time, the family grew to include Calvin, born in 1972, and another son, Joseph, born in 1975. Joseph was taken away by the Department of Social Services, and Steve believes an Ontario family adopted him.

Steve landed a job repairing small motors at a resort in Loon Lake. The relative prosperity that came with steady employment, however, did little to improve the family's circumstances. "On pay day we used to drink and then we'd fight." With such turmoil in their lives, it was only a matter of time before Social Services intervened again. The couple agreed to send Calinda to live with Bernice and Pete Martel on the Flying Dust Reserve near Meadow Lake, and Calvin to live with a woman named Madeline Okimow. Not surprisingly, Steve and Margaret seldom saw their offspring. Occasionally, the youngsters would visit for a few days, but then they would return to their foster homes.

Pete and Bernice Martel usually had two or three foster children at any given time, and their daughter Evelyn remembers the kids being "spoiled rotten." Evelyn has mostly positive memories of Calinda Waterhen's stay with her family in the early 1980s. "She was quite quiet and liked to sit around and read those true story books and watch TV. Her favourite show was *Happy Days*. Calinda liked the romantic, mellow music that they played in the eighties." Calinda dreamed of becoming a teacher, and it never occurred to Evelyn to doubt that the skinny girl with the free spirit and quiet determination would realize her goals. "I thought she was going to go somewhere and do something better," says Evelyn. But the most important thing to Calinda "was to be part of a family. That's what she wanted more than anything." Calinda seemed to be happy at the Martels for the most part, but there were lonely periods, too, and she often ran away. Sometimes she returned to Loon Lake. But she was always brought back.

By 1983, the common-law marriage of Steve Morningchild and Margaret Waterhen was over. That same year, in Calgary, Steve met Georgina Lonechild, a woman from the White Bear First Nation in southeast Saskatchewan. The new couple drank to excess, following the old patterns, until something oddly dramatic occurred. On December 27, 1983, after drinking for two days straight, they suddenly decided to "quit living like this," as Steve puts it, "and that was it. We quit drinking and I haven't drank since."

Steve found work as a carpenter and began rebuilding his life. But for Margaret, who had moved to Saskatoon, it was too late. Her drinking continued until she died. In 1984, her body was found in an alley behind the Baldwin Hotel, a downtown bar that has since disappeared from the landscape but in its heyday was infamous for its violence and clientele. According to street rumours that made their way back to Steve Morningchild in Loon Lake, Margaret had died of an overdose.

For all intents and purposes, Steve Morningchild had lost his two eldest children, at least in terms of having a daily influence on their lives. At the same time, he knew they were in capable hands, being raised by guardians he trusted. In common with First Nations people in general, Steve Morningchild did not find it necessary to possess or control his children. He did not think of himself as irresponsible; rather, he believed that an extended family would ensure that the people who were best suited to look after the needs of Calinda and Calvin were doing just that.

It was in late 1992 and into the spring of 1993 that Steve Morningchild became seriously worried about Calinda. In April 1993, there were two family funerals in Loon Lake within days of each other. Calinda did not show up for either, a fact that Steve found troubling. He went to the local RCMP detachment in May 1993, worried that something had happened to his daughter. He was assured that she was alive and living somewhere in Saskatchewan.

"The officer told me that her health card was being used, but since she was over eighteen they couldn't tell me her location, even though I was her father."

In October 1994, Steve heard reports from Saskatoon that the remains of three women had been found southwest of the city. He wondered if one of the women could be Calinda, since he knew she had been living in Saskatoon and the family had had no contact with her for two years. Again he went to the RCMP.

"They said, 'no, no, she's still alive and according to the law we can't tell you where she is.'" Evidently, Calinda's health card was still being used by someone, somewhere in Saskatchewan. "I said, as a father, I have a right to know where she is. What about my law?"

On Friday, the 13th of January 1995, Steve Morningchild got his answer.

Corporal Jerry Wilde, the media relations officer for the RCMP in Saskatoon, issued a two-paragraph news release, confirming that Calinda Waterhen had been positively identified through dental records as the third victim found in October 1994. The release went out to the Saskatoon media in mid-afternoon, but it was embargoed until six o'clock the next morning.

In Loon Lake, Steve Morningchild opened the door and greeted an RCMP officer.

"I want to talk to you outside," the officer said. Morningchild followed him out to his police cruiser. "I'm sorry to inform you that your daughter is one of the women whose body was found down near Saskatoon," the officer said.

"I started screaming at him," Steve remembers. "I wanted to get out of the car and beat the shit out of him. They lied to me all this time. Why didn't they look into it when I asked them?"

Coincidentally, perhaps, but almost certainly by design, the identification could not have come at a better time for the police. In the Saturday edition of the Saskatoon *StarPhoenix*, a front-page story announced: "Police discover woman's identity." A copy of that day's paper was placed in the motel room at the Imperial 400 where Bill Corrigan was preparing to meet John Martin Crawford for the third consecutive night. The RCMP hoped Crawford would make some incriminating statement as a result of seeing the story in the paper.

Steve Morningchild has become a spiritual man. He participates in traditional ceremonies and regularly consults with Elders in an attempt to better understand the teachings of his people.

"Our religion keeps us going," he explains. "We pray to the

Creator, we pray for people who have passed on with alcohol and drugs in their system or have committed suicide."

At Calinda's funeral, Steve learned from an Elder that her spirit would advance to the other side without delay, since her life had been taken from her. The Cree believe that spirits that are unclean, as a result of drugs or alcohol in the body at the time of death, are destined to spend a period of time in a place resembling purgatory before they move on to the other side.

"If somebody ends your life on Earth, you move to the other side," said Steve Morningchild. "John Crawford took the load off her by killing her."

Chapter Ten

"A Friendly Mother of Four"

"I've been called squaw *lots of times. It kind of grew to a point where I have anger toward white people. After this happened to Eva my anger grew, even though I know you can't blame a whole race for the actions of one man."*

–Bev Taysup
April 2000

Mary Taysup and Oliver Okemahwasin were determined to raise their eleven children in a more sheltered environment than the Yellow Quill Reserve could offer. In the 1960s and '70s Yellow Quill, near Kelvington in eastern Saskatchewan, had earned the dubious reputation of being a place where police officers hoped they would never be posted. Violence and alcohol abuse were widespread. Housing was inadequate. Many children rarely attended school.

As a child, Bev Taysup remembers, she was not allowed to go

out much, or to keep company with other children on the reserve. Her mother and father, she says, "didn't want us around kids whose parents drank a lot and ran wild."

She struggles to speak Saulteaux, the language of her mother, as she and Mary Taysup look back on the family's early years.

"At the time, I thought they were being over-protective, but now I understand. They wanted the best for us. We never went hungry, and we always went to school."

At twenty-nine, Bev is the fourth child, seven years younger than her sister Eva, who was murdered by John Martin Crawford in 1992.

Among the happiest times mother and daughter remember were the warm Saskatchewan summer days when the family travelled to powwows in the area. Bev remembers her bigger sister running off to play with the older girls, her loud laughter carrying throughout the grounds. Eva was a gregarious girl, always smiling, and usually surrounded by friends.

The family moved away from Yellow Quill as Mary and Oliver attempted to shield their brood from the pitfalls of reserve life. They settled for a time in Kelvington, then for a while in the small hamlet of Nut Mountain. It may have done some good, but by the time Eva was seventeen she was showing definite signs of rebellion. Mary and Oliver's rules were too strict for her. She ran away—first to Wynyard, then, a day or two after she had been brought back from Wynyard, to Saskatoon, where she moved in with a cousin named Brandy.

Soon after moving to Saskatoon, Eva met Ian Gardypie, a young man from the Beardy's and Okemasis First Nation near Duck Lake. They moved in together. In 1983 thirteen-year-old Bev Taysup, after a year at St. Michael's Residential School in Duck Lake, moved to Saskatoon to live with them. In 1985 Eva gave birth to a little girl whom they named Rene. Three other children followed in rapid succession: Sydney in 1986, Rickie in 1988, and Angel Dawn in 1989.

Bev thought that her sister occasionally became frustrated looking after the children, she was so young herself. Her mother quietly contradicts her in Saulteaux: "She looked after her kids really well."

Bev's recollections of those years are of her sister raising "her little family," with a steady stream of friends dropping over for coffee and long visits. Eva loved to have company, and with four youngsters to care for, she didn't get out very often.

"Her smile was so big and she had a loud laugh," Cheryl Taysup remembers, speaking fondly. Cheryl, a first cousin to Eva and Bev, was perhaps ten or eleven when she used to visit Eva and the children. "She had a real nice personality. When I was there she was taking care of the kids, and I remember she would include all the kids in everything, and make sure they shared."

The oldest child, Rene, is a pretty, open-hearted girl with her mother's eyes and smile.

The pressures of raising four children with inadequate resources took its toll on the parental relationship, and by 1991 Eva and Ian were living apart. The family was split further when Rene and Rickie went to live with their grandparents, while Sydney and Angel Dawn stayed with another aunt, Coreen.*

According to Bev, Eva fell heavily into the party scene after she and Ian separated. Perhaps she was trying to make up for lost time. Her favourite haunt was the bar at the Barry Hotel, where there was live music in the evenings and she could be around her friends. She loved to dance.

"My sister was an outgoing person," says Bev. "She loved to be around people. She was a trusting person, sometimes too trusting." But even though Eva would often bring home strangers when Bev was living with her, Bev is convinced she was not a prostitute.

The two sisters spent New Year's Eve of 1991 partying at the Barry Hotel. As the two women drank and danced the night away, Eva told Bev: "1992 is going to be a good year for me." They made plans to put their lives on track in the New Year.

* In 1998 thirty-three-year-old Ian Gardypie, the father of Eva Taysup's four children, was found in an alley behind a house on the west side of Saskatoon. He had been beaten severely. His skull was fractured, and he had sustained serious internal injuries. He died in hospital. Brian Cote, April Cote, and Brenda Cote later pleaded guilty to manslaughter in the death. April Cote and Ian Gardypie had had a child together before separating.

For Bev, 1992 would be a good year. She had a new man in her life, Greg Edmunds, a musician from Pittsburgh. She had met him when his band was playing a gig at the Barry. The band toured throughout Canada and the United States in 1992, and Bev was with him.

Eva's New Year did not go as well. In mid-January, she called her parents, who were living in Saltcoats, a small town in southern Saskatchewan.

"She was crying and scared, but she wouldn't say why," says Mary. "She wanted us to come to Saskatoon to get her."

Never affluent, it took Mary and Oliver two weeks to raise the money to make the trip. When they arrived in Saskatoon, Eva was nowhere to be found.

"It wasn't like her to just leave and not tell anybody," says Bev, who called home several times over the next few months, asking if anyone had seen her older sister. No one had.

The Taysup family went to the police in Saskatoon, Kelvington, and Yorkton. They filed missing person reports, complete with recent photographs of Eva. No public announcements followed, no requests for information as to the whereabouts of Eva Taysup. The family heard nothing for almost two years.

A cousin later told a *StarPhoenix* reporter that she had seen Eva some time in March, and that she had not cashed her March welfare cheque. Ian Gardypie's younger brother, Donny, thought he had seen Eva in Calgary. The family tried to remain optimistic, but to Bev it didn't make sense: "She had four kids that she loved; she wouldn't just up and leave." Bev kept her own counsel, although "deep down I knew there was something seriously wrong."

As the months turned into years, Mary Taysup also began to lose hope, and frequently cried herself to sleep. Indeed, eight years after losing her daughter, Mary still cannot conceal her grief. She removes her glasses to brush the tears from her eyes as she describes in Saulteaux a dream she had about Eva's funeral before they knew what had happened to her.

When the first body was found in October 1994, Bev was afraid that the remains might be those of her sister. Her concern deepened when two more sets of remains were found three weeks later.

On November 16, 1994, less than a month after finding her body, the RCMP made a positive identification. Dental records confirmed that the body was that of Eva Taysup, who had been missing for more than two years. John Crawford's affidavit has him meeting Eva in the Barry Hotel sometime in September 1992, but that does not jibe with the Taysup family's belief that Eva went missing in March that year.

The Saskatoon *StarPhoenix* ran a front-page story under the headline, "Friendly mother of four among murder victims."

According to Bev, the family felt some relief at finally knowing what had happened to Eva, but "there was a big emptiness" even so.

The tragedy has taken an emotional toll on Bev, although she has found a measure of peace and stability in her life. Her relationship with Greg Edmunds, a multi-talented saxophonist, flutist, and keyboard player with a Saskatoon-based blues band, is solid. The couple has a beautiful daughter. And Bev has returned to school. But in many ways the "big emptiness" remains.

"I already had a negative attitude toward white people," she admits. "Growing up in a little town, I ran into a lot of prejudiced people. I've been called *squaw* lots of times. It kind of grew to a point where I have anger toward white people in general. After this happened to Eva my anger grew, even though I know you can't blame a whole race for the actions of one man."

Chapter Eleven

LUCKY TO BE ALIVE

It will be up to the courts to decide if the Mounties acted appropriately . . .

John Martin Crawford met and had sex with countless women during the six years he lived in Saskatoon. Many were prostitutes he picked up in downtown bars or working the streets of Pleasant Hill or Riversdale. He had a knack, too, for enticing defenceless women into his car. Generally they were intoxicated, or otherwise unable to recognize the dangers. Most, if not all, of the women he targeted were Native. It is the nature of the predator to go after the weak, and he seemed to know instinctively that Native women working the street were particularly vulnerable.

Given his perennial pursuit of sexual gratification, it is likely that Crawford crossed paths with several hundred women between 1989 and 1995. The least fortunate—Shelley Napope, Eva Taysup, Calinda Waterhen, and perhaps others—

were murdered. Others, including Louise Alice LeMay and Melanie Fiddler, were lucky to escape with their lives.

Incredibly, there are even more tales to be told, few of them more disturbing than that of Theresa Kematch. Crawford picked her up one night in October 1994. Theresa claims that he beat her, raped her, and left her on the street. What made this attack different from others Crawford may have committed is that members of the RCMP had Crawford under surveillance at the time, which raises the issue of the extent to which the police actually witnessed what happened to Theresa.

Less than a week after the first set of human remains was discovered in the grove southwest of Saskatoon, investigators were discussing the possibility that John Martin Crawford might be responsible. A surveillance team was immediately assembled. Surveillance work can involve hours of mind-numbing watching and waiting, and often the results fail to justify the investment in costs and manpower. This was not the case with Special O, the surveillance team set up to watch John Martin Crawford. It was spectacularly successful.

The plan was to begin watching John Crawford, virtually every day, starting at around 4:00 PM and continuing throughout the evening until 8:00 or 9:00 PM, and occasionally later. Depending on the availability of personnel, the team would include between five and nine members.

On October 11, the first surveillance team hit the streets. They followed Crawford in his mother's grey 1986 Mercury Cougar as he made his rounds. It was approaching eight o'clock when he spotted Theresa Kematch, a young Native woman. She was extremely, and obviously, intoxicated. She could barely keep her balance. Crawford pulled up beside her, and she got in. Theresa recalls leaving a house party that night not far from where she met Crawford, but she doesn't remember what, if any, conversation took place before she accepted a ride from him. When she got into the car, she was well over half the city away from her parents' east-side home in Sutherland, but she was only three or four blocks from her sister's apartment on Avenue R South.

Crawford, of course, had no intention of taking her to either location. He made an abrupt turn and headed down Avenue P toward Garfield Street, where he had taken Louise LeMay and perhaps many others. With the surveillance vehicles following at a discreet distance, Crawford pulled into the storage lot behind Vern's Car Wash on 11th Street. Navigating a well-worn, pot-holed track through the septic tanks, culverts, and other concrete detritus, he managed to park the car out of view of the nearby intersection. He turned the engine off and climbed into the back seat with Theresa.

Theresa doesn't remember much of what happened that night. She isn't sure where the incident occurred or how long it took, "but I remember him putting his hand on my throat and pulling at my clothes. He raped me. I can remember the smell of sex. I can't get that out of my head."

From a distance, RCMP officers watched the scene unfold, exchanging information on their police radios. Testimony given by Corporal Bob Todd at the preliminary hearing suggests that two officers in particular may have been close to the Crawford vehicle while the attack took place. But it has yet to be determined what they were able to observe. Police picked up Theresa later as she staggered past a PetroCanada bulk station on 11th Street, her jeans open, her face cut and swollen.

She was placed under arrest.

Surveillance co-ordinator Corporal Bob Todd and his boss, Sergeant Colin Crocker, took the young woman into the back seat of their unmarked car and headed downtown. After a brief stop at the city police station on 4th Avenue, Todd and Crocker took Theresa across the river to the RCMP detachment on the east side. There she was examined by a matron and lodged in a cell. Not surprisingly, she remembers nothing of either the stop at the city police station or the examination. She does recall waking up in the morning—massively hung over, one assumes—to discover that her underwear was missing. About 9:30 AM, after a futile interview in which Todd had hoped to learn something that might assist the Crawford investigation, Theresa was driven to within a block of her parents' home in Sutherland and released. She had been in police custody for approximately thirteen hours.

That the attack on Theresa Kematch had occurred while John Crawford was under surveillance by the RCMP first came to light at John Crawford's preliminary hearing in June and July 1995. Todd was the first of two officers to be cross-examined by Crawford's lawyer, Mark Brayford. Brayford gave him a rough ride. After a two-week break, it was Crocker who took the stand, this time to answer questions from Hugh Harradence, the other member of Crawford's defence team. Crocker, who had just returned from a training session in Ottawa, had evidently not discussed the matter with Todd before taking the stand, for the investigators' responses to the different lawyers' questions were often at odds. Both agreed that Theresa Kematch had been highly intoxicated when they came upon her at the PetroCanada station, but then their recollections diverged. To quote the transcript from the preliminary hearing:

> *Brayford:* Was Theresa hurt in any way?
> *Todd:* She did not appear to be. She was not bleeding if that's what you mean, or bruised.

Two weeks later, Crocker's exchange with Harradence painted a somewhat different picture:

> *Harradence:* Your witness evidence summary, Sir, indicates that you came upon an individual that had been badly beaten?
> *Crocker:* That's correct. I was with Corporal Todd at the time.
> *Harradence:* Thank you, Sir. Could you elaborate on what you mean by badly beaten?
> *Crocker:* She was sitting on the curb, holding her head, and she was crying and appeared to have some swelling about the eyes.
> *Harradence:* Did she appear to have black eyes, Sir?
> *Crocker:* I couldn't tell whether it was black eyes or not.
> *Harradence:* Broken nose?

Crocker: There appeared to be some swelling.

Harradence: I see. And how close did you get to her, Sir?

Crocker: I was within a couple feet.

Harradence: Okay. And there was definitely some injury to her that was readily apparent to you?

Crocker: Yes, Sir.

Harradence: And would have been readily apparent to anyone in the vicinity?

Crocker: Yes, Sir.

Harradence: And, Sir, you formed a belief, Sir, that she was potentially the victim of a sexual assault?

Crocker: Of an assault for sure.

Harradence: Sir, would it be correct to say that your witness evidence summary indicates that "We spoke to this person and realized that she had been sexually assaulted by the person in the vehicle?"

Crocker: That was relayed to me by another person.

Harradence: Did you speak to [Theresa]?

Crocker: I did, and I believe that the matter of the sexual assault was relayed to me by another member.

"Another member" was most likely the officer whom Crocker acknowledged was within "ten feet" of Crawford's car when the attack took place. Why the RCMP did not move in to prevent the assault is a question that has yet to be answered satisfactorily. John Crawford had killed before. The RCMP knew it, and they had reason to believe he might be responsible for at least one other killing. Theresa was in a car with a suspected sexual predator and a known killer.

Theresa had refused to proceed with any assault charges when interviewed by the police. She didn't breathe a word to her parents. She told only one person about the attack: her sister. Like many victims of rape, she felt both shame and disgust. Following the attack by John Martin Crawford, Theresa crawled into a shell of her own making and started to drink even more. The pattern will be recognizable to any social worker or psychologist: she entered into abusive relationships, attempted suicide, and frequently drank to the point of unconsciousness. Finally, at the urging of family members, she began seeing a psychiatrist. It was only then that she was able to discuss the events of that first night of Special O.

Almost six years after the rape, Theresa sought the help of Saskatoon lawyer Ron Piche. He subsequently filed a statement of claim on her behalf with the Court of Queen's Bench in Saskatoon, alleging that the RCMP was negligent in its duty to protect Theresa Kematch from a man it knew to be a sexual offender and who had been convicted of manslaughter. The suit alleges that Theresa's rights under the Canadian Charter of Rights and Freedoms—specifically Section 7, which states, "Everyone has the right to life, liberty and security of the person and the right not to be deprived thereof except in accordance with the principles of fundamental justice"—were violated when the RCMP failed to prevent the attack. The suit is also based on Section 15(1): "Every individual is equal before and under the law and has the right to the equal protection and equal benefit of the law without discrimination and, in particular, without discrimination based on race, national or ethnic origin, colour, religion, sex, age or mental or physical disability."

Theresa Kematch is a dark-haired, brown-eyed woman of obvious Native ancestry. Admittedly, the RCMP was trying to build a case against a possible serial killer and Theresa had entered the car of her own free will, but the question must be raised: had she been a white woman, would the police have permitted John Crawford to take her to such a place and subject her to potential danger?

Ron Piche, who has successfully sued the RCMP in the past in a case involving an aboriginal woman, alleges that the police strategy was flawed at this stage. Rather than warning the public that a dangerous sexual predator was cruising the streets of Saskatoon, the police were preoccupied with building a case against their suspect, even if it meant putting innocent people at risk. The RCMP sees it differently. Its Statement of Defence filed in Saskatoon's Court of Queen's Bench for Saskatchewan on September 8, 2000, disputes certain facts presented by Piche and disavows any wrongdoing on the part of the officers involved in the surveillance. The statement concludes: "The RCMP were not aware of the time of death or racial origin of the human remains found outside Saskatoon until after the incident involving the plaintiff and Crawford. The information linking Crawford to a possible homicide was not reliable. The RCMP was aware that Crawford had been convicted of a manslaughter charge and had served his lawfully imposed sentence. . . . the police do not have a legal duty to warn the public about any person who has been previously convicted of a violent offence. There was limited information available to the RCMP at the time, and they did not know that [Theresa Kematch] was a potential target or that the plaintiff was at risk from Crawford."

Piche cites a 1998 Ontario Court decision supporting his view. In *Jane Doe versus the Board of Commissioners of Police for the Municipality of Metropolitan Toronto et al* a Toronto woman successfully sued the Metropolitan Toronto Police Force after she had been attacked by a serial rapist. In the early morning of August 24, 1986, the plaintiff, known only as Jane Doe, was raped at knifepoint by an assailant identified in the action as PDC. He broke into her apartment in the Church and Wellesley area of Toronto, through the balcony. She was the fifth victim of the man who became known as the "Balcony Rapist." PDC had been committing similar crimes in apartment residences in the area beginning on New Year's Eve 1985 and continuing throughout 1986. By the time Jane Doe was raped, the police had decided that the crimes were related. They also believed that the assailant lived in the same area, and that he was a serial rapist who attacked women who lived alone in second- and third-floor apartments with accessible balconies. They had also deduced that he would almost certainly strike again, likely around the 24th or 25th of the month. The crimes received virtually no publicity; the two officers assigned to the case issued no public warnings. The officers later testified that they had not wanted to alert the public to the danger because they did not wish the assailant to flee, as had the "Annex Rapist" in a similar case some time previously.

In ruling in favour of the plaintiff, Madam Justice Jean MacFarland stated:

> The police are statutorily obligated to prevent crime, and, at common law, they owe a duty to protect life and property. The police force failed utterly in their duty to protect the plaintiff and the other victims from a serial rapist known to be in their midst by failing to warn them so that they might have had the opportunity to take steps to protect themselves. A meaningful warning could and should have been given to the women who were at particular risk. This warning would not have compromised the investigation. The professed reason for not providing a warning, that is, that the assailant might flee, was not genuine, and the real reason was that Sergeants C and D believed that women living in the area would become hysterical and scare off the offender and this would jeopardize the investigation. Sexist stereotypical views . . . caused the investigation to be conducted incompetently. Had a warning been given, the plaintiff would have taken steps to protect herself and likely those steps would have prevented her from being raped.
>
> The plaintiff's Charter rights were infringed by police conduct. The police investigation was carried out in a way that denied the plaintiff equal protection and equal benefit of law as guaranteed to her by Section 15(1) of the Charter. The conduct of the investigation and, in particular, the failure to warn was motivated and informed by the adherence to rape myths as well as sexist stereotypical reasoning about rape, about women, and about women who were raped. The plaintiff was discriminated against by reason of her gender.

Justice MacFarland awarded Jane Doe $175,000 in general damages, $37,301 in special damages, and future costs of $8,062, for a total of $220,363.

The Ontario case and Theresa Kematch's Statement of Claim appear to have some elements in common. For example, Crawford's attacks regularly began in the eight-block area where he picked up his victims; similarly the "Balcony Rapist" committed his crimes in a specific locale. In her claim, Theresa Kematch argues that the Jane Doe case is similar to hers because of issues of discrimination: gender in the Jane Doe case and race in the Kematch case. As well, in the Ontario case, neither the RCMP nor the Saskatoon Police Service made any attempt to warn potential victims that they were in danger. Both cases give rise to the question of the appropriateness of police conduct.

The RCMP Statement of Defence challenges a number of statements contained in Theresa Kematch's Statement of Claim. Rather than picking up Theresa on 20th Street, as the Statement of Claim states, the police say they observed John Crawford picking up Theresa at the door of the Albany Hotel. After a brief stop at a residence on Avenue N South—most likely Jimmy Mason's house—Crawford took the woman to the concrete yard location. There, amongst the cement culverts and weeds, one officer got close enough to Crawford's Cougar to see John and Theresa engaging in intercourse. According to the officer, "partway through the sexual act, [I] observed Crawford straighten up and he appeared to be either slapping something and/or swinging his arms around." The officer moved closer to the vehicle, hoping to get a better look and discern what was happening. Suddenly Crawford got out of the car and pulled Theresa out of the back seat. He got back in his car and sped away, leaving Theresa on the ground. The officer made no contact with Theresa, but returned to his vehicle as the woman stumbled through the weeds and debris before making her way to Avenue P, where she encountered Sergeant Crocker and Corporal Todd. The police, the Statement of Defence maintains, had no opportunity to intervene during this brief period of observation, and Sergeant Crocker insists that if the police had believed that anything serious was happening, they would have stepped in to stop it.

As for Theresa's condition when Crocker and Todd picked her up, Paragraph Seven of the Statement of Defence appears to contradict the court testimony of Colin Crocker and the witness evidence summary he had penned. "There was no indication that she required medical attention, and the plaintiff denied needing medical attention when the same was offered to her. The plaintiff did not appear to have any visible marks, cuts, or bruises." Theresa, who had not been co-operating with the officers, had been beaten. Crocker confirmed this at Crawford's trial when the police officer had been questioned about the incident. He also noted the swelling around her eyes and nose.

The RCMP is downplaying its suspicions regarding John Martin Crawford at the time of the attack on Theresa and the possibility that Crawford had been involved in the death of a woman known only as "Angie." This information, supplied by its informant, Bill Corrigan, is described in the Statement of Defence as "limited and not reliable." It was, however, intriguing enough for the Mounties to assemble a surveillance team within days and begin a concerted observation of Crawford.

Following, as it does, in the wake of the Jane Doe case in Ontario, and given the somewhat contradictory testimony of the RCMP officers, Theresa Kematch appears to have a strong case. But it is far from open-and-shut. Her laywer has several legal obstacles to negotiate, not the least of which is the RCMP's contention that the claim contravenes *The Public Officers Protection Act* and *The Limitations of Actions Act*.

It will be up to the courts to decide if the Mounties acted appropriately; whether they should have known that John Martin Crawford—who had served time for manslaughter, had a record of violence, and was a suspect in a suspicious death— posed a danger to Theresa and the general public.

Chapter Twelve

THE MEDICINE MAN'S VISION

"I rode with the spirits to Saskatoon . . . I saw your niece . . .

What I saw next is very wicked."

—Medicine man Clifford Youngbear

A chance meeting with a medicine man in the summer of 1992 convinced Elmer Lonethunder that his niece, Shirley, had not simply walked away from her family. He believes she may have been murdered.

Elmer was attending a powwow at Fort Qu'Appelle when it happened. It was a three-hour drive from his home on the White Bear Reserve near Carlyle in southeastern Saskatchewan, but the gathering was usually well worth the effort and expense of getting there. Elmer loved to watch the dancers in their colourful costumes and listen to the skilful drummers, many of whom had travelled long distances to compete, or simply to entertain. The atmosphere beneath the vast prairie sky was one of fellowship and good spirits, and on such occasions Elmer's ancestral pride and optimism were strong. But this time he was finding it hard to concentrate. Other thoughts were intruding on his mind.

Only six months earlier, the Lonethunder family had learned that one of their members had mysteriously disappeared. Shirley Lonethunder, last seen on December 22, 1991, left a six-year-old daughter, Delilah, and a baby boy, Talon, who celebrated his first birthday on Christmas Day. By all accounts, Shirley loved to party, and she had occasionally worked as a prostitute in Saskatoon. But according to her sister, Lorna Lonethunder, it was entirely out of character for her to leave her children, particularly since it was just three days before Christmas. She had gone Christmas shopping at Midtown Plaza in Saskatoon, and hadn't been seen or heard from since. There were no clues. The family had no theories about where she might have gone. It didn't make sense.

Elmer Lonethunder's values and concerns were consistent with those of any devoted uncle. The fact that Shirley had occasionally worked as a prostitute in Saskatoon no doubt caused him grief, but that was no reason to withdraw his affection. A single Native woman from the reserve, uneducated and for all practical purposes unemployable, has few career options. Often the street is not the easiest, but the only way out. Elmer understood these things very well; if anything, his understanding increased his concern for his missing niece.

He was mulling these things over when he felt a tug on the sleeve of his denim jacket. He turned to see an old man standing beside him. "Somebody in your family is missing," the old man said.

Startled, Elmer asked the stranger to repeat what he had said, although he had heard it well enough the first time.

"I've been watching you, and I can see you are troubled."

With the respect due to an Elder, Elmer gently inquired who the old man was. The man identified himself as Clifford Youngbear, a medicine man from Poplar, Montana, a community

Mug shot of John Martin Crawford taken in 1992, the same year he was charged with raping Janet Sylvestre. *RCMP photo*

John Martin Crawford is led into the Saskatoon courthouse for his trial in May 1996. *Warren Goulding photo*

Mary Jane Serloin as a young girl (third from the right in the second row) in a class picture. Even by this age, Mary Jane had experienced her share of tragedy. She was killed by John Martin Crawford in 1981. This is one of the few photos salvaged by the family after a house fire. *Justine English photo*

Victoria Crawford arrived alone at the Court of Queen's Bench in May 1996. She spoke to no one during the trial and entered the courtroom to take a seat directly behind her son. *Warren Goulding photo*

Bill Corrigan (right) leaves the courthouse accompanied by Constable Al Keller. Corrigan was the key witness in the Crown's case against John Martin Crawford. *Warren Goulding photo*

John Crawford's defence lawyers, Hugh Harradence (left) and Mark Brayford, enter the courthouse for the May 1996 trial. *Warren Goulding photo*

Sergeant Colin Crocker headed the RCMP team in the Crawford murder investigation. *Colin Crocker photo*

Art Larson, the Lethbridge lawyer who represented John Martin Crawford in 1982. *Warren Goulding photo*

Moon Lake area, where the remains of Shelley Napope, Calinda Waterhen, and Eva Taysup were discovered. Arrows point to locations of the remains. *RCMP photo*

Dr. Ernie Walker in the morgue at the University of Saskatchewan. It was Dr. Walker, working with little more than skeletal remains, who helped police identify the three Saskatoon victims. *Warren Goulding photo*

Janet "Smiley" Sylvestre, late 1980s. To date, her murder remains unsolved. *RCMP photo*

Composite sketches by Cyril Chan of the remains of the victims based on the findings of Ernie Walker. (Top to bottom) Shelley Napope, Calinda Waterhen, Eva Taysup. *RCMP photo*

(Top to bottom) Shelley Napope, Calinda Waterhen, Eva Taysup, early 1990s. *RCMP photos*

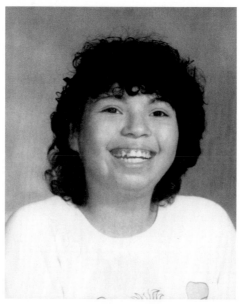

Shelley Napope, age thirteen. *Hubert and Merle Napope photo*

Hubert and Merle Napope at a mass for their daughter Shelley, December 1994. *Greg Pender/StarPhoenix photo*

Eva Taysup, age sixteen. *Mary Taysup photo*

Eva Taysup's younger sister, Bev (left), with Eva's daughter Rene and Eva's mother, Mary Taysup. *Warren Goulding photo*

Calinda Waterhen, age sixteen (right), poses with her brother Calvin (left) and their father Steve Morningchild. *Steve Morningchild photo*

Patrick Asapace, Shelley Napope's uncle, expressed anger that Bill Corrigan did not do more to protect his niece. *Warren Goulding photo*

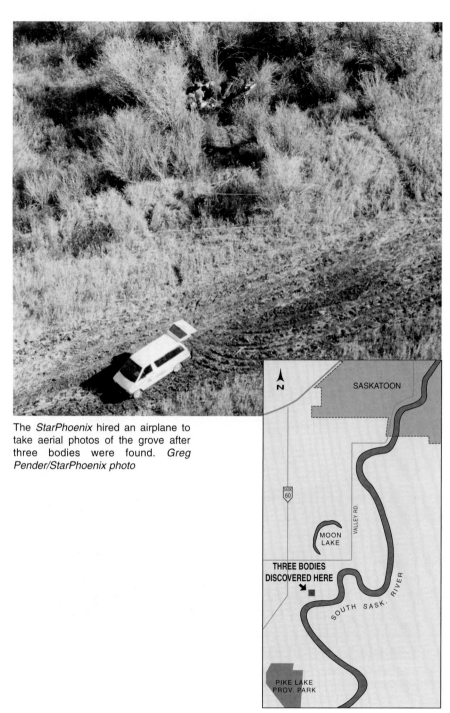

The *StarPhoenix* hired an airplane to take aerial photos of the grove after three bodies were found. *Greg Pender/StarPhoenix photo*

SASKATOON

N

SASK 60

VALLEY RD.

MOON LAKE

THREE BODIES DISCOVERED HERE

SOUTH SASK. RIVER

PIKE LAKE PROV. PARK

Map of area where the bodies were found. *Brian Smith*

Saskatoon author and professor Janice Acoose (left, with her arms around her niece) and Carol Dalton (middle) participated in a prayer vigil following the trial of John Crawford. *Warren Goulding photo*

The grove in which the bodies of Eva Taysup, Calinda Waterhen, and Shelley Napope were found contained many signs that Native Elders used the area for religious ceremonies. Ribbons hung in the trees, and fruit cans had been placed on the ground as offerings. *Warren Goulding photo*

StarPhoenix reporter Donella Hoffman interviews Crown Prosecutor Terry Hinz after John Crawford had been convicted of one count of first-degree murder and two counts of second-degree murder. *Warren Goulding photo*

Victoria Crawford's 1986 Cougar was used regularly by her son as he made his nightly rounds picking up women. *Warren Goulding photo*

on the Fort Peck Indian Reservation in the northeastern part of the state.

"I know things people normally don't know," he said matter-of-factly. His voice, at once husky and soft, conveyed a sincerity that could not be doubted. "I can see this is hurting you. You better do something about it."

Elmer promised Clifford Youngbear that the family would do all they could, but they didn't know where to start. Implicit in the statement was a request for advice, but the old medicine man said nothing else. Elmer was too respectful to press him. Deep in thought, Elmer drifted over to a gathering of tents where men were playing games of chance. They weren't using cards or dice, but sticks or bones, sometimes feathers. Such hand games, a traditional test of skill, speed, and luck, are staple fare at powwows. With complex strategy and eye-blinking speed, players try to outwit one another and acquire all the sticks. The games can go on for hours, the stakes growing higher by the minute. At one time men would walk away from a game having forfeited their horses and valuables, perhaps all their possessions. No doubt some would have bet their homes as well, but the tipis traditionally, and perhaps wisely, belonged to the women. With so much at stake, the game can be almost as engrossing to the spectator as to the participant. But for Elmer Lonethunder that afternoon, the diversion held little of its usual appeal. His encounter with Clifford Youngbear was deeply troubling. What could he do? Saskatoon was a long way from White Bear. Certainly, he felt a sense of responsibility to his sister Doris and to his niece, Shirley, but he didn't know where to turn.

A week later, Elmer crossed the border into Montana with Shirley's mother, Doris. His purpose was twofold. First, the annual Standing Bear powwow on the Fort Peck Reservation was highly regarded across the west, and one was surely advised to take it in if possible. Second, and more important, Elmer wanted to talk to the medicine man again and introduce him to Doris.

The campground was filled to capacity with campers and trailers, while tents, including brightly decorated tipis, had been pitched beyond the parking area. There were people from all over the western United States and Canada, including dancers from Arizona and New Mexico, and craftspeople who followed the powwow trail every season selling leather goods and beaded clothing and other wares. Bannock sizzled in blackened pans hanging over fire pits, and the air was rich with the fragrance of buffalo burgers and savoury stews emanating from the concession area. Youngsters frolicked in the grounds, making new friends. Some collected drink cans and juice bottles, hoping to earn enough money to buy a handful of candy or some other treat. One thing they wouldn't find was beer bottles or cans. Alcohol was strictly forbidden.

Elmer searched the sea of unfamiliar faces for the medicine man. He caught sight of him at a favourite spot, near the gate where the dancers would gather for the Grand Entry. Clifford Youngbear was smiling at the little girls attired in their colourful jingle dresses, at the little boys making last-minute adjustments to their costumes, and at the older boys and young men who were putting on their most serious faces in readiness for the competition that would follow.

Elmer and Doris made their way through the crowd, walking carefully around the outside of the circle. The dancing area is sacred, reserved for the dancers and other guests only when they have been invited to participate.

The medicine man saw them approaching. He extended a hand to Elmer. "Good day, my friend."

Elmer introduced Doris, the mother of his missing niece.

"My daughter's Indian name is Flying Around Woman," Doris told him in English, then in Cree, a language the Montana medicine man did not know well. "I believe my daughter is alive, but I must know what has happened to her. Can you help us?"

Youngbear is often called upon to help families when relatives are ill or experiencing other problems, and readily agreed to help. There were no formal arrangements to be made, no contract, no exchanging of phone numbers, just the word of an old man who promised to speak to God on behalf of a family from Saskatchewan.

That was what Elmer and Doris had come to hear. They were satisfied. They knew they would meet the medicine man again.

Clifford Youngbear's Siouan name is Iron Gourd. He is the grandson of Iron Woman, one of the most revered medicine women of her time. It was from his grandmother that young Iron Gourd learned the spiritual ways of the Dakota people. Iron Woman schooled him in the ceremonies and traditions of their people, and the art of herbal medicines. By the time he was eight, Clifford Youngbear had attained the status of medicine man, a position of esteem, and one that his generation regarded as sacred and beyond reproach. Almost sixty years later, Youngbear acknowledges that the role and prestige of the modern medicine man has diminished, at least in the eyes of the young.

"The young people only know whisky, wine, and beer," he laments. "They don't understand what I am doing. People are mean to me. They are jealous of me."

Despite the skepticism he sees all around him, Youngbear remains constant in his belief that God will guide him and show him things that other people cannot or will not see: "I am always asking God for help. That is why I can do things that the doctors can't do. With God's help I can do many things."

After meeting Elmer and Doris at the Standing Bear powwow in July 1992, Youngbear did what he always did, and followed through on his promise: "I asked God to tell me what had happened to this woman."

The following spring, Elmer Lonethunder again met Clifford Youngbear at a powwow, this time at White Shield, North Dakota. It had been more than a year since Shirley had disappeared, and no one—family, friends, police—had any answers. The medicine man, however, had news. As is the custom, he allowed Elmer to draw it out of him, until finally the old man told Elmer of the vision he had experienced.

"I rode with the spirits to Saskatoon," he said. "We rode down the streets of Saskatoon. There we saw stores, a supermarket, maybe. I saw your niece. She was with two men. Then we rode out of Saskatoon to the southwest, I think it would be . . ." The medicine man hesitated. "What I saw next is very wicked."

"You must go on," Elmer persisted. "We need to know what happened to Shirley."

The old man spoke softly. "She has no worries now. She's dead. The two men pulled her out of a car and roughed her up. One man, he raped her. Another guy, a big guy, he did the killing. Then they threw her into a hole."

He did not see Shirley's face, but he knew it was she. "I called her name and whoever was there answered." The men's faces were unclear to him.

"Here, I'll show you where she is at." The medicine man picked up a flattened popcorn box. Tearing it open, he began to sketch a crude map on the cardboard. "There are bushes between two lakes," he said. "One lake is shaped like a C and the other is like an E. The place is seven, maybe eight miles from Saskatoon. That is where you will find her."

"There are other bodies there," the medicine man added, almost as an afterthought. "I am certain of that."

It did not occur to Elmer Lonethunder to disbelieve the medicine man. Nothing that has happened since has altered his opinion. That meeting with Clifford Youngbear in the summer of 1993 took place some fifteen months before the remains of Eva Taysup, Calinda Waterhen, and Shelley Napope were discovered in a grove southwest of Saskatoon—a grove, oddly enough, sandwiched between the crescent-shaped Moon Lake to the northwest and the meandering South Saskatchewan River to the south and east.

Clifford Youngbear's vision, though terrible, brought Elmer Lonethunder a degree of comfort. At least he knew, finally, what had happened to Shirley, and perhaps the family was a step nearer to closure. He returned to White Bear with the news. And while most family members did not question the medicine man's vision, Doris Lonethunder wasn't yet prepared to accept that her daughter was dead. She, too, had been seeking spiritual advice, and had been told that Shirley was alive and would return to the family when she turned thirty on January 3, 1996.

It wasn't an easy thing for Elmer Lonethunder to decide that the police needed to know what Clifford Youngbear had told him. He was aware that few, if any, would believe him. As his niece Lorna, Shirley's sister, reminded him, "A white person doesn't know what we know."

Nevertheless, he made an appointment to see an RCMP officer in Carlyle. Fortuitously, it turned out to be Louise Bear, a Native constable who had been with the force for less than three years. In Constable Bear he found a sympathetic ear and an understanding spirit. She listened to the account of Clifford Youngbear's vision, comfortable with the notion that the medicine man from Montana who had never set foot in Saskatoon was being forthright in his claim of having seen a woman being murdered and buried near Saskatoon. She herself had been taught not to dispute the power of the medicine man. At the same time, she knew there were charlatans in the world of the shaman, as there are in any other. She believed in medicine men "who are able to see things and explain in detail what they see." Clearly, Clifford Youngbear met those criteria. At the same time, however, Constable Bear was hardly in a position to march in to her superior officer and demand action on a Saskatoon murder investigation based on the vision of a Montana medicine man. She filed a report and let the matter take its course.

"I wish I could have done more," she told a *StarPhoenix* reporter six months after the remains of Taysup, Waterhen, and Napope were discovered. That was almost two years after she had first learned of Clifford Youngbear's vision.

In late April 1995 the Saskatoon daily published a front-page story on Shirley Lonethunder's disappearance. Although the young woman had been missed in the downtown area where she worked as a barmaid and occasional prostitute, it was not public knowledge that Shirley was a missing person. As with Eva, Calinda, and Shelley, and who knows how many others, the police made no appeals for public assistance, no posters were taped to lampposts. The *StarPhoenix* story, in fact, was the first acknowledgement that Shirley Lonethunder had been missing since December 1991 and that her family, including two young children and a distraught mother, missed her desperately and wanted to see her walk back into their lives.

At the RCMP detachment on 8th Street, officers ridiculed the article, suggesting the *StarPhoenix* was indulging in *National Enquirer*-style journalism. It was another year before they admitted that they knew Shirley Lonethunder was missing, that she was, in police parlance, quite likely the victim of foul play, and that John Martin Crawford was a suspect in her disappearance and probable murder.

On April 12, 1995, under the headline "Grove may harbour more bodies," the *StarPhoenix* published an interview with Constable Al Keller, who mused about the logistics of excavating the grove in which the bodies of the three victims had been found. It would be a huge task given the fact that all the trees and the thick growths of willow would have to be cleared, and the soil carefully removed.

"We've taken a lot of steps in that direction," offered Keller. The constable was a key member of the GIS team, but he didn't often talk to the media. "We haven't done a full excavation and upturned the land," he said, but that was something to be considered: "What else do you do if the bodies are buried two feet down and are completely covered and there's been growth over top of them? We have to satisfy ourselves that that isn't the situation."

It would be a mammoth task, Keller conceded, but there were good reasons for at least considering it: "We haven't had a lot of families saying they reported their daughters missing, but it's fair to say that we've got one or two that we're concerned about.

"Just because we have charged Mr. Crawford at the moment," Keller concluded the interview, "it doesn't mean we're not examining every other possibility and the fact that there may be other bodies."

It is not in Al Keller's nature to deal in half-truths. When he spoke of plans to undertake a more comprehensive search of John Crawford's dumping ground, he was speaking from the conviction that it would eventually be necessary. He knew there were women whose whereabouts were unknown, and he was very much afraid that they had suffered the same fate as Eva, Shelley, and Calinda. He also had files on Shirley Lonethunder and another young woman named Cynthia Baldhead, who has not been seen for more than nine years. He had real concerns that they, too, had been murdered. He couldn't reveal their names to the media, but that didn't stop him from demonstrating that he cared enough to consider excavating the entire grove.

The idea didn't play well at the detachment on 8th Street. Four hours after the *StarPhoenix* story hit the street, the Mounties issued a terse denial in the form of a three-sentence news release. There was no indication, they claimed, that there were any other bodies at the location where the three women had been found. "We are not excavating and have no plans to excavate at the above or any other site," stated Corporal Jerry Wilde, the Saskatoon Sub/Division's crime prevention co-ordinator and media liaison officer. The paper had been scolded, and so had Al Keller, who was reminded that Wilde was the only officer authorized to speak to reporters.

Wading in late, the electronic media in Saskatoon took delight in reporting the RCMP's outrage at the previous day's *StarPhoenix*, hinting broadly that the daily paper may have embarrassed itself by running a non-story.

More than a year later, and literally hours after John Crawford had been convicted of killing Shelley Napope, Calinda Waterhen, and Eva Taysup, Sergeant Colin Crocker told *Maclean's* magazine that when the first skeletal remains were uncovered in October 1994, police assumed the victim was Shirley Lonethunder: "Hers was one of the first names given to us and I thought for sure it would be her."

Talon Lonethunder turned nine on Christmas Day, 2000. He has no memory of his mother He has been raised mostly by his aunt, Lorna Lonethunder, and his grandmother Doris. His older sister, Delilah, is now fifteen.

More than eight years after Shirley Lonethunder went Christmas shopping in downtown Saskatoon, police are no closer to laying charges. John Martin Crawford remains their prime, if not their only, suspect. They have made repeated attempts to discuss various cases with him, but Crawford's not talking.

Chapter Thirteen

SHE CRIED RAPE

"I still have Janet Sylvestre on my mind after all this time."

—Sergeant Colin Crocker

RCMP Sergeant Colin Crocker is convinced that John Martin Crawford killed Janet Christine Sylvestre. So is Crown prosecutor Terry Hinz. Even Bill Corrigan believes that Crawford is lying when he denies killing thirty-seven-year-old Janet Sylvestre in October 1994. Add to this an eyewitness who saw Janet Sylvestre in the company of two men and had the sense to write down the licence number of their car, and the case against the multiple killer takes on legal substance. The motive—not that Crawford ever needed one—has been obvious since Sylvestre, a Dene woman originally from La Loche in northern Saskatchewan, complained to police that Crawford had raped her in 1992. Crawford, for his part, complained to police that Janet had threatened him later that year.

At Crawford's murder trial in 1996, the strength of the

RCMP's suspicions was made clear. In a *voir dire* examination Mark Brayford, Crawford's lawyer, read an excerpt from an affidavit written in the fall of 1994 by Constable Al Keller in support of an application to secretly tape conversations between John Crawford and Bill Corrigan. A *voir dire* examination is heard out of the presence of the jury, who may otherwise be influenced by what they hear before the trial judge has ruled on the admissibility of certain evidence. The affidavit said, in part: "Based on the totality of the information believed to date, I believe that Crawford and [Jimmy Mason] are both involved in the killing of Shelley Napope and Janet Sylvestre."

Six years and three convictions later, John Martin Crawford has not been charged with the murder of Janet Sylvestre. Nor has anyone else. The file was turned over to Corporal Rick Torgunrud of the major crimes unit of the RCMP in Regina in early 2000. It was felt that a fresh look at the six-year-old case was needed. Since receiving the file, however, the unit has made little progress. By late April 2000, Corporal Torgunrud had managed only a cursory review of the Sylvestre file. But that was enough to tell him that the case was replete with unanswered questions and unsolved puzzles.

Investigators began their surveillance of John Martin Crawford on October 11, 1994. The Special O team spent several hours watching their suspect that first night. It proved to be an eventful tour that included Crawford's attack on Theresa Kematch. Day two was cut short when Crawford went home around 9:00 PM and Sergeant Crocker decided to call off the surveillance for the rest of the night. It is a decision he has been second-guessing ever since. On Thursday, October 13, the body of Janet Sylvestre was discovered beside a grid road sixteen kilometres west of Saskatoon. She was naked. A plastic bag covered her head. An autopsy later revealed that she had been asphyxiated.

"With the benefit of 20/20 hindsight, maybe I would do things differently," Crocker says today. "I still have Janet Sylvestre on my mind after all this time." The source of his conflict, of course, is the possibility that Crawford didn't stay home the night of October 12, but headed downtown in his mother's car after the surveillance team shut down operations.

Two women watched from the intersection near the Barry Hotel and claim that Jimmy Mason grabbed Janet Sylvestre by the arm and forced her into a dark grey 1986 Cougar that was parked across from the hotel on Avenue B. Another man, whose features they couldn't make out, was in the driver's seat. One of the witnesses was Shirley Gardypie, who knew both Sylvestre and Mason from the downtown scene. She wrote down the plate number as the car pulled away and turned onto 20th Street. After hearing of Janet's death a few days later, Gardypie went to the police and, somewhat reluctantly, reported what she had seen, including the plate number, DMF 594. The car was registered to one Victoria Crawford, of 113 Avenue Q North, Saskatoon.

Six years later, though, Shirley Gardypie's memory seems to be failing her. She is no longer certain what time of day she saw Janet with Jimmy Mason. It may even have been in the afternoon, before the evening's surveillance had begun.

"I know it was busy in the bar, and there was a band playing," she says. "I wish I could be put under hypnosis, then I could be sure."

That the bar was packed and there was live music would suggest that it was later in the evening. Further, if it had been daylight, the two witnesses should have been able to get a better look at the driver of Victoria Crawford's car. Common sense points to the obvious—it was John Martin Crawford—but common sense and the obvious are frequently inadmissible in a court of law. Shirley Gardypie's statement was sufficient, however, to arrest Jimmy Mason for kidnapping. It was January 19, 1995, the same night John Crawford was charged with the murders of Eva Taysup, Shelley Napope, and Calinda Waterhen. The case against Crawford for the killing of these women was solid, but there wasn't enough evidence to charge either Mason or Crawford with the murder of Janet Sylvestre. Mason was arrested. Shirley Gardypie had identified him. The prosecution hoped they would be able to get the whole story from Crawford's friend.

Mason certainly told stories. He talked for more than three hours, all of it videotaped by the RCMP. When it was over, the Mounties were left shaking their heads and Crown prosecutor Terry Hinz was extremely frustrated. With the threat of a murder charge on the table, Mason admitted to having taken Janet Sylvestre to his house where John Crawford proceeded to rape her and then beat her unconscious, whereupon the two men took her from the house and drove out into the country. But then Mason changed his mind.

"He basically told the police that a woman was beaten to death at his house," says Hinz, "then he changed his mind and said, 'No, that didn't happen.'" Further, his description of the plastic bag that had been placed over Janet's head was inaccurate. In the end, police didn't know what to make of his evidence. In Hinz's colourful language, "It was sickening, watching him slither all over the frigging room. At the end of the day we didn't think anything [Jimmy Mason] had to say was worth a pinch of coon shit." He was such a "screw-up," according to Hinz, "that we eventually cut him loose."

Jimmy Mason left Saskatoon before Crawford's trial in May 1996 and headed for another western Canadian city, where he soon became a fixture in that city's skid row, frequenting the soup kitchens and seedy bars. But before leaving, Mason agreed to an interview with the *StarPhoenix*. He used the opportunity to try to convince the reporter that he was a pretty swell guy, despite what the police thought.

"I knew Janet Sylvestre well," he declared. "The lady stayed at my house and drank. Lots of young ladies have been to my house, and I've helped them out lots of times and never done any harm to them." A fifty-some-year-old bear of a man, his unkempt greying beard brushing the table in front of him, Mason was enraged that the police had arrested him and played hardball with him for several hours. "I'm talking to my lawyer, and I'm going to try and sue the cops."

As for Shirley Gardypie, Hinz has "no reason to call her a liar, but there is some reason to believe that she may have been mistaken."

Bill Corrigan's role in the apprehension and conviction of John Martin Crawford was crucial. Without his information and co-operation, Crawford might have eluded the police for some considerable time. Corrigan was well compensated for his efforts, though he admitted having been present during the murder of Shelley Napope. He even went so far as to concede that it was his knife that had been used to slay the teenager. In normal circumstances, he might have been a co-accused, or at least an accessory after the fact. Instead he was paid $15,000 plus expenses and managed to sidestep a major prosecution for theft in the Albany Hotel incident.

But Corrigan couldn't avoid being dragged into the Janet Sylvestre murder. Mark Brayford's aggressive cross-examination of the informant in the final moments of John Crawford's triple murder trial in 1996 raised some interesting questions. Corrigan denied that he had been in Saskatoon on October 12, 1994—the night Janet Sylvestre was killed—but he couldn't provide a convincing alibi. According to a private detective Brayford had hired, Corrigan wasn't at work in Winnipeg that day. Further, a Saskatoon woman, Cori Mayes, maintains to this day that she saw Corrigan in the company of Janet Sylvestre in a downtown bar the night Janet was killed. Bill and Janet had been good friends, according to Corrigan himself.

"I've given Janet a place to stay, helped her with money," Corrigan told a journalist shortly after his trial testimony. "There's no way I would ever hurt Janet. I broke down and cried when I first heard she had been killed."

Corrigan claimed that he felt some responsibility for Janet Sylvestre's death, as he had been pressing her for information in 1992 and 1993 regarding the death of Shelley Napope. If Janet had been nosing around for information that Corrigan could turn over to the Mounties, she might well have been in danger, particularly if it got back to John Crawford. "I knew what John had done to her previously," Corrigan said, referring to the alleged rape in May 1992.

When the RCMP were clandestinely recording Corrigan's conversations with Crawford in January 1995, the informant had given his friend every opportunity to admit to the murder of Janet Sylvestre. Crawford had not hesitated to describe what he had done to Shelley Napope, Eva Taysup, and Calinda Waterhen, but he consistently denied killing Janet.

"When I asked him about it he was giggling and laughing, and he said no," Corrigan told the reporter. "I think he's lying. The way he said 'no' tells me either he was involved or he knows who did it."

True, Janet's body was dumped several kilometres from the bodies of Shelley, Eva, and Calinda, but the circumstances were not dissimilar. "Other than a few minor things," Corrigan noted, "it falls into John's M.O."

But if John Crawford killed Janet Sylvestre, as almost everyone close to the case seems to think, why did he deny it? One theory suggests that he feared the large Sylvestre clan. The rape charge in 1992 had drawn him to their attention, and he had good reason to fear for his safety, either on the street or behind bars.

Janet was one of eighteen siblings. For the last few years of her life she was not particularly close to her brothers and sisters, and she was also estranged from her children. At the time of her death in October 1994, Janet's son Lorne, a grade twelve student, was being raised by her older sister, Toni Lemaigre, in La Loche. Her daughter, Crystal, was living with a brother, Jules, also in La Loche. Toni says that Janet phoned often to check on the children, but La Loche is seven hours by road from Saskatoon, and she hadn't made the trip for a while.

She had been moving around. Toni knew she had been in Winnipeg recently and that she had lived in Edmonton for a time. In Saskatoon, she lived in a tiny apartment on Avenue D South, two blocks from the Barry Hotel. Her sister Geraldine, younger by three or four years, had a room in the same building.

One of Janet's closest friends in the six months prior to her death was Marcy Nault, a former taxi driver, now an addictions counsellor. "People call me the Butch Indian," she says matter-of-factly. Nault took Janet under her wing, but their relationship was not sexual. Janet spent much of her time in downtown bars, particularly the beverage room of the Barry Hotel. They called her "Smiley." Most people enjoyed her manner, but Marcy says that Janet's trusting ways often got her into trouble: "She took too many chances. When she needed a ride, she'd get in a car with anybody. I tried to stop her. I told her to call me any time she needed a ride. I'd come and get her. She didn't always listen."

The day before she died, Janet had made plans to have dinner with Marcy. Her friend recalls: "I told her I needed some knives so I could cook Chinese food, and she went out and bought some for me. I got the vegetables and what I needed for sweet and sour, and we were looking forward to the meal. I saw her earlier that day. Then I never saw her again."

Janet and her sister Toni had been close at one time. They had been raised by an aunt, while the other Sylvestre children grew up with their natural parents. But Janet became more and more aloof from Toni as the years passed: "She used to keep her private life to herself. She wouldn't share anything with me."

Effectively shut out of Janet's life, Toni acquired tidbits of information where she could. She had heard about Janet's brush with death in Edmonton when someone pushed her out of a moving car. But she hadn't heard about the rape charge in 1992.

As the months and years have passed and no one has been charged with killing her sister, Toni Lemaigre has become philosophical about it: "Whoever is the person that did it, they're in their own prison. I don't want to dwell on it. I have better things to do."

Building a case against John Martin Crawford may become easier with the establishment of a national DNA data bank under the *DNA Identification Act*. The legislation, which will allow police to take blood samples from offenders convicted of certain offences and store them in a central data bank, will also enable prosecutors to apply for permission to take blood samples from previously convicted offenders.

"Mr. Crawford," Terry Hinz says dryly, "is a prime candidate." Indeed, if the police found tissue or body fluid from the killer on Janet Sylvestre's body, it could be compared with DNA from a suspect, and "We just could be a few months away from matching Crawford definitively with Sylvestre."

A great deal of time has passed, but the file is not quite cold yet. The Mounties have a suspect—perhaps two suspects—and physical evidence from the crime scene together with the new *DNA Identification Act* may finally provide the means to build a case against their prime suspect and bring some closure for the family and friends of Janet Sylvestre.

Fourteen

On Trial

"We're going to get this guy."

—Crown prosecutor Terry Hinz

By the time John Martin Crawford arrived at Queen's Bench Court to face three counts of first-degree murder, more than sixteen months had passed since his arrest, and more than two years since the bodies of Eva Taysup, Calinda Waterhen, and Shelley Napope had been found. It had been four years since the three women first disappeared. The wheels of justice had been turning slowly. They were about to accelerate.

For a trial that promised to uncover the lurid details of a triple sex murder, interest in the proceedings was decidedly low. Unlike the Paul Bernardo trial in Toronto the previous summer, there were no line-ups of the curious hoping to catch a glimpse of Canadian crime at its most brutal. Nor was there any need to frisk the spectators for concealed weapons. With the exception of a handful of reporters and family members, and two regular court watchers—a pair of jovial retired men who regularly attend for entertainment and mental stimulation—no one seemed interested enough in the case to take it in.

It was a cool May in Saskatoon. Spring had been slow to arrive after a brutal winter. But despite the lingering cold, the ambience was serene. On the west bank of the South Saskatchewan River, the stately old Spadina Crescent courthouse stood in the shadows of the venerable Delta Bessborough Hotel. The park across from the courthouse was coming to life with lush dark grass. The elms lining Spadina were beginning to leaf out. There was a sense of renewal. It was a stark contrast to the grim proceedings that were about to begin in Courtroom No. 1.

The trial began on Tuesday, May 21, 1996, the day after the Victoria Day long weekend. But a key preliminary argument had already been settled three weeks earlier when Crawford's legal team appeared before Mr. Justice David Wright in an attempt to have the twelve hours of taped conversations between their client and Bill Corrigan disallowed as evidence. Mark Brayford and Hugh Harradence knew that the tapes were essential to the Crown's case; as such, they were also critical to any defence they hoped to muster. The passage of time had erased almost all physical evidence at the scene of the murders. Police questioning of Crawford following his arrest had yielded little, largely because of Brayford's perennial advice: "Don't say anything." It's the same advice he gives all his clients: be polite, but don't say anything that may incriminate you. It is unlikely that Crawford needed much in the way of counsel for dealing with the police. He had played this game before. In a videotaped conversation with Constable Al Keller not long after he was brought into the detachment, Crawford refused to be drawn into any of the investigator's traps. He may not have been the brightest client Brayford had ever represented, but he was pragmatic. He knew the system.

The morning after Crawford's arrest and appearance in provincial court, Crown prosecutor Terry Hinz gave Mark Brayford a thorough briefing on what the Crown had on his client. The conversation likely brought little joy to the defence attorney. According to Brayford, "It is not a happy day when you see Terry Hinz with a case as strong as the one they had against John Crawford." Brayford characterizes Hinz as "a very formidable opponent. He has the best knowledge of the law of any prosecuting counsel in this province."

When the two squared off three weeks before the actual trial was to begin, Brayford was at a decided disadvantage. But he is a man of no mean reputation himself. He based his argument on Section 24(2) of the Canadian Charter of Rights and Freedoms:

> Where . . . a court concludes that evidence was obtained in a manner that infringed or denied any rights or freedoms guaranteed by this Charter, the evidence shall be excluded if it is established that, having regard to all the circumstances, the admission of it in the proceedings would bring the administration of justice into disrepute.

Brayford hoped to convince Mr. Justice Wright that the police had not been adequately forthcoming in their description of the investigative techniques they planned to use when applying for permission to set up the wiretaps. Specifically, they had failed to reveal to Mr. Justice Gerein, who had authorized the wiretap, certain important details about the surveillance of John Crawford in early October.

Details of Crawford's attack on Theresa Kematch while the surveillance team hovered nearby were contained in an affidavit prepared by Corporal Charles Jeffrey Keyes and supplied to Mr. Justice Gerein along with the wiretap application. The team's inaction was certainly open to question, Brayford said. If they were going to let someone who had committed a sexual assault continue to roam the streets, then "it is logical and reasonable for the public to expect that they would maintain intensive visual surveillance." But what took place on night two of the surveillance was even more problematic. When Crawford returned to his mother's home on October 12, 1994, the surveillance team assumed that he was home for the night and withdrew. But several hours later Janet Sylvestre had been seen in the company of two men who roughly forced her into a car that happened to be registered to Victoria Crawford. One of the men had been identified as Jimmy Mason, one of John Crawford's frequent companions. In the affidavit prepared for Judge Gerein, Corporal Keyes stated that circumstances would suggest that Crawford might well be responsible in the death of Janet Sylvestre. But Mr. Justice Gerein, Brayford argued, didn't have the whole story.

"The critical thing that was not placed before the authorizing judge, and we suggest deliberately," Brayford said, "was the fact that they had John Crawford under surveillance on the 12th and discontinued surveillance at nine o'clock in the evening. They followed him home and simply made a decision; well, that's enough for today.

"This affidavit," he continued, "is diligently trying to paint a picture that my client killed Janet Sylvestre. But they have left out the fact that they had him under surveillance that evening."

Would Mr. Justice Gerein have deemed it necessary to grant a wiretap authorization if he had had the option of judging whether or not other investigative techniques were unlikely to succeed? He should have been given all the facts.

"We suggest that the absence of that full and candid disclosure of what occurred on October 12th points to something that, if His Lordship had been aware of it, he would not have issued the authorization. Perhaps," he concluded, "it's a little embarrassing that they discontinued surveillance on the suspect and a couple of hours later someone is killed."

Terry Hinz countered the defence argument, which he characterized as "horribly flawed." The suggestion that more intensive surveillance might have caught Mr. Crawford in the act of other crimes completely missed the point. "The point was, what will it take to solve the murder of this young woman whose bones were found bleaching in the sun from an incident that happened two years earlier? The fact that the police may have caught Crawford in the act of even another murder would have provided no evidence at all as to whether or not he was the culprit in relation to the earlier victim."

Hinz provided half a dozen precedents to back his position,

and concluded that "to throw out the key evidence against a multiple murderer based on a technical violation would not only bring the administration of justice itself into disrepute, but would cause outright public outrage."

Brayford visibly bristled. "I would point out to the public and to this Court," he said, "that at this point my client is simply an accused person."

Wright reserved his decision, opening the door for the lawyers to continue the debate on the first day of the trial. But on May 21, the first order of business was to select a jury. The process took less than forty minutes. When it was over, six men and six women were sworn in and watched intently as Cindy Ritchie, the court clerk, rose to speak.

"John Crawford, you stand charged as follows:

"John M. Crawford, of the City of Saskatoon, in the Province of Saskatchewan, stands charged that between the first day of January, AD 1992, and the 31st day of December, AD 1992, at or near Saskatoon, in the Province of Saskatchewan, he did:

"Count #1—did commit first degree murder on the person of Eva Taysup, contrary to Section 235(1) of the *Criminal Code of Canada*.

"Do you understand the charge as read to you?"

Crawford, who had been ushered into the courthouse through the back door ten minutes before court was to begin, muttered his response: "Yes."

The clerk continued: "How say you, do you plead guilty or not guilty?

"Not guilty," Crawford replied, staring at the floor.

The procedure was repeated twice more as Crawford was charged with first-degree murder in the deaths of Shelley Napope and Calinda Waterhen, then Ritchie turned her head and reported to Judge Wright: "Not guilty, My Lord."

Crawford's physical appearance had altered somewhat since the preliminary hearing. His hair and moustache were neatly trimmed, and he was wearing a blue crew-neck pullover with broad grey stripes over a cream-coloured shirt. His demeanour, however, was consistent with his previous court appearances: an expression as flat as his voice, and a look of indifference that edged on boredom. Occasionally he glanced over at his mother, Victoria, who was invariably staring back at him from her seat a few feet away.

With the critical issue of the wiretap evidence still undecided, Wright excused the jury and the proceedings moved into *voir dire*. Constable Al Keller was called to the stand to describe the technical aspects of the process; Brayford's apparently uninspired cross-examination was aimed only at bringing out details that could be used later to discredit the tapes and transcripts. Constable Tom Steenvoorden, who had been part of the surveillance team, was called to add more facts, then Hinz and Brayford picked up where they had left off three weeks before. In mid-afternoon Mr. Justice Wright ordered a brief adjournment to consider counsels' submissions. He retired to his chambers, and returned shortly with his decision. The jury would hear the tapes. They would hear John Martin Crawford's own voice, and, unless the defence was able to convince the judge to exclude the transcripts, they would also read his blunt account of the killings in black and white.

Brayford was philosophical. "Our argument would have worked if this were a drug case," he said later. "It isn't. It's a murder case. You don't win murder cases on technicalities."

The jury was recalled and Mr. Justice Wright gave them the standard instructions, outlining their role and responsibilities. The jury would not be sequestered. He then turned the floor over to Terry Hinz.

Hinz is at home in the courtroom. His strong voice and powerful presence belie the appearance of a bespectacled, somewhat frail-looking man with a beard and thinning brown hair. His mind is agile, and he's quick to cut to the chase. Part of his charm is his ability to put legal pretence aside and use a more common vocabulary. Moments before the preliminary hearing began, he leaned over a courtroom divider and apologized to members of one of the victims' families for the "pretty yucky stuff" they were going to have to listen to. He described the interior of Victoria Crawford's car, on which "these forensics people will spend many happy hours," as "wall-to-wall semen stains."

Born and raised in Prince Albert, Saskatchewan, Terry Hinz graduated from the University of Saskatchewan law school in 1976, articling in the legal department at the City of Saskatoon under Brosi Nutting, Chief Judge of the Provincial Court of Saskatchewan until January 2001. He prosecuted his first murder in 1979, the worst year on record for homicides in Saskatoon. Since then he has recorded more first-degree murder convictions than any other prosecutor in the province. In fact, he has lost only one—in 1986, when Cindy Caron was found not guilty of killing Laura Ahenakew. Caron had been represented by Gerry Allbright, now a Queen's Bench Justice and the man who defended wife-killer and former Saskatchewan cabinet minister Colin Thatcher.

Hinz's success rate, perhaps, owes as much to his attitude as to his skill. Inevitably, he says, your ego is involved. "If you think a guy is guilty, you hate to lose. You look in the mirror and you have to be able to say, 'I presented the case professionally. I gave it what I could.'" At the same time, he refuses to buy into the hype and glamour of murder: "There's nothing all that special about a murder case. Murders are assaults where somebody died. The stakes are a little higher, that's all." Even so, "If the next crime victim is your sister," he says, "you'd want me to prosecute."

"We're going to get this guy," Hinz had promised Shelley Napope's family.

Hinz was well prepared to prosecute John Martin Crawford. Once the question of the tapes was out of the way, the Crown prosecutor was ready to begin a methodical tendering of the evidence. He began by outlining the Crown's case and detailing how he was going to proceed over what he expected would be a five-day session. At this stage of a murder trial, the prosecutor is given ample leeway to reveal details of the investigation and explain how information pointing to the accused was gathered. Actual testimony must come from witnesses, but the prosecutor is permitted to predict what the jury will hear in the course of the trial.

"Much of the evidence in this case is going to be unsettling," he told the jury. "We are talking about three murders. Much of the evidence consists of tape-recorded conversations. The language is vulgar from time to time, explicit."

He held nothing back. He described the discovery of the bodies of Calinda Waterhen, Shelley Napope, and Eva Taysup. He detailed Bill Corrigan's role in the investigation. He outlined the work done by Dr. Ernie Walker, the University of Saskatchewan forensic anthropologist who was able to determine the victims' identities. He described Crawford's forays into the neighbourhoods frequented by prostitutes. He told the jury of the plan to bring Corrigan back from Winnipeg and use him to set up the murderer. The resultant twelve hours of tape, he said, were rife with shocking comments and crude details.

The first witness to be called, appropriately, was Brian Reichert, the man who had literally stumbled across the skull of Calinda Waterhen in what has come to be known as the Moon Lake district. His discovery reopened an investigation that had stalled a year earlier, and investigators began to believe there was something to the tale Bill Corrigan had fed them in 1993.

Next in the witness stand were two RCMP officers. Corporal Clarence Tuck described how he had photographed the scene, taken measurements, and left markers where bits of evidence were found. His evidence was straightforward. Brayford asked only three questions in cross-examination.

Allan Gillis, a sergeant with the Forensic Identification Section, didn't get off so easily. Gillis had taken dozens of photographs, including aerial shots, of the three crime scenes. Among the more gruesomely useful exhibits were the shots he had taken of the shallow grave where Eva Taysup had been buried. Because there had been a crude attempt to bury the body, more of it remained. Gillis's photos documented the investigators' painstaking removal of the corpse under the direction of Dr. Ernie Walker. The skull and other bones were clearly visible, as well as a blanket, and an orange electrical cord that Crawford had used to bind the body. The remains were placed on a sheet of plywood and taken to Royal University Hospital where Dr. Walker undertook a more complete examination.

Hugh Harradence was itching to get at a specific aspect of Gillis's testimony. Harradence, who grew up under the tutelage of a father with the reputation of being one of the most ferocious cross-examiners in western Canada, lobbed half a dozen preliminary questions at Gillis, then he got to the point: "With respect to the third site, specifically in relation to the media, Sir, had they beat you there?"

Gillis replied in the negative, adding that the reporters and photographers who were present at the scene were being shepherded by Corporal Jerry Wilde, the RCMP's media relations officer. Harradence persisted. He wanted to know how close the reporters had come to the third crime scene. Near enough, Gillis conceded, that he and other officers working there could hear their voices and see them clearly. Harradence was hoping to undermine the integrity of the holdback evidence—the electrical cord and blanket. Had the media seen these items? Had they later reported on them? The cross-examination was inconclusive, but the issue would be revisited later.

Mr. Justice Wright adjourned the proceedings for the day.

Before the jury was called the following morning Terry Hinz and Mark Brayford wanted to discuss the implications of similar-fact evidence, an issue the judge would be forced to rule on before the trial moved much further. It had been revealed at the preliminary hearing that the Crown had assembled more than one story from alleged victims of John Crawford. These women, all Native, told of having been picked up by the accused, usually choked and beaten, and always forced to have sex. Miraculously, they had survived to tell their stories. Their evidence, Hinz argued, spoke volumes about what John Martin Crawford was capable of. Only the victims he left alive could give the jury some idea of the atrocities that may have been committed on the dead. Defence lawyers, not surprisingly, routinely argue that such testimony is critically prejudicial to their clients. Judge Wright decided to put it off for another day, and the lawyers agreed to move forward with testimony from two key RCMP witnesses on condition that they would not be required to answer questions related to similar-fact evidence until after Wright had ruled on its admissibility.

Terry Hinz called Corporal Robert Todd. At the preliminary hearing, it was Todd, the long-haired undercover officer, who had described Crawford's attack on Theresa Kematch when police had Crawford under surveillance. As the issue of similar-fact evidence had yet to be ruled on, his testimony at the trial was not nearly so dramatic. Hinz posed a handful of questions dealing with the discovery of the third set of remains. Brayford had no questions at all.

Todd's boss, Sergeant Colin Crocker, was called to the stand. Crocker's evidence, too, was circumscribed and cautious. The jury did not hear about the attack on Theresa Kematch. Nor did they hear about Crocker's decision to lift the surveillance on the night Janet Sylvestre was murdered. Those matters would have to wait for another day.

Anticipating Harradence's line on cross-examination, Terry Hinz led Crocker through a description of his role at the murder scene, zeroing in on the media's appearance. Crocker testified that the holdback evidence—the electrical cord and blanket—was not visible to the media, and that later he had succeeded in keeping that evidence from them. Crocker had spoken frequently with the media, and he had monitored what was being reported in the newspapers and the electronic media. He was confident that no one besides the on-site officers and Dr. Ernie Walker—and the murderer, of course—knew about the blanket and the electrical cord.

Hugh Harradence rose to cross-examine. He got down to business immediately: "Sergeant Crocker, at any time have you been reprimanded about your involvement with the media in relation to this case?"

"Define a reprimand for me, Sir."

"You don't understand the word reprimand, Sir?"

"I have not been reprimanded for it, no."

"You have been criticized about your involvement with the media?"

"Yes, Sir," Crocker conceded.

Inspector Andy Murray at the Saskatoon detachment had evidently become concerned about Crocker's burgeoning rapport with the Saskatoon media. In the absence of Corporal Jerry Wilde, the media relations officer, Crocker had often fielded questions from reporters. Even when Wilde was on duty, Crocker and other officers regularly entertained questions from a *StarPhoenix* reporter. Inspector Murray had little to worry about. The adept Crocker had managed to keep the media well away from the actual investigation.

But Harradence did not particularly care about that. He was keen to re-focus on the holdback evidence. His reasoning was simple. In the taped conversations with Bill Corrigan, John Crawford had talked about the cord and the blanket—information only the killer of Eva Taysup could have known. But if Harradence could demonstrate that that essential bit of knowledge was widely known, the defence might be able to tender the theory that Crawford had learned about the cord and blanket by reading the newspaper or watching television. It was a stretch, to be sure, but Brayford and Harradence were looking for any opening they could find.

Harradence took Crocker back to the crime scene. How close had the media been? What about the airplane the *StarPhoenix* had hired to fly over the scene to take photographs? Had television cameras been able to zoom in on the body? Crocker remained cool and steadfast. There was no way the media had captured the holdback evidence on film. There was no way he or any of his officers had revealed essential details to any of the reporters they spoke with during the three-month investigation. For their part, the jury seemed unimpressed, even if they did understand the significance of Harradence's aggressive cross-examination. They retired to the jury room with puzzled looks as Mr. Justice Wright ordered a mid-morning break.

Corporal Jerry Wilde was next on the stand. In May 1996, Wilde had been the media relations officer at the Saskatoon RCMP detachment for almost six years. It's a job he continues to hold today. He enjoys the work, and he's managed to nurture a relationship with the local media that is comfortable, sometimes even cozy. He is accessible, quotable, and sympathetic. He understands the media, their idiosyncrasies, their insatiable appetite for information. But, as with all successful corporate communicators, Wilde can only reveal what he knows. If his bosses aren't inclined to provide him with all the information, Wilde cannot be expected to have all the answers. Just how much Jerry Wilde had been kept in the dark in the John Martin Crawford investigation was made clear on day two of the trial.

Terry Hinz asked him first if he was familiar with the term "holdback evidence." Corporal Wilde responded that he was, "somewhat." When asked his understanding of the term, Wilde replied, "It's evidence that's not released to anyone, be it the media or any other people that are not involved in the investigation."

Hinz continued: "And as of October 23, 1994, were you aware of whether there was any holdback evidence in this case?"

Wilde replied without hesitation. "There was not."

"Were you made aware at any point that there was?"

"I don't recall that, no."

When asked if he had been told about the circumstances in which Eva Taysup's body had been found—specifically, the blanket and the electrical cord—Wilde admitted that he had not been privy to that information. Indeed, he had not become aware of it until after the preliminary hearing. Clearly, if anyone had learned about the holdback evidence, it hadn't been from Wilde.

The morning concluded with the introduction of a document signed by John Crawford and Mark Brayford, agreeing that the remains found by Brian Reichert and the RCMP were those of Calinda Jean Waterhen, Shelley Napope, and Eva Taysup. This allowed the Crown to release this evidence—the remains—to the families since the identity of the victims would not be raised as an issue by the defence.

As was the case at the preliminary hearing a year earlier, the role of Dr. Ernie Walker was to describe in scientific detail the circumstances under which the skeletons of Shelley Napope and Calinda

Waterhen and the slightly more complete remains of Eva Taysup had been discovered in October 1994. Armed with a tray of slides, the renowned forensic anthropologist led the jury through the steps he had taken, beginning with the finding of the remains of Calinda Waterhen. He pointed out the fibrous covering of the bones, called periosteum, the ligamenta structures still apparent.

"These materials did give off an odour," he said matter-of-factly, indicating "something rather recent."

He attributed the scattering of the bones to carnivore chewing. Coyotes, foxes, and domestic dogs had obviously found the remains first.

The jury was enthralled. Some grimaced at the images on the screen. Others covered their mouth. Occasionally, someone would scowl at the accused, hunched over in the prisoner's box. For some members of the victims' families, it was too much. At one point, Merilyn Napope sobbed loudly and fled the courtroom. Crawford was unmoved. He glanced up infrequently. Mostly, he stared at the floor. If Walker's exposition bothered Crawford in any way, he did not show it.

Walker's testimony continued for almost two hours. He explained how he had been able to determine the race, approximate age, and various physical characteristics of the dead women. In the first two cases, where bones were virtually all that remained, he had still managed to determine how many years they had lain on the ground. He could not, however, determine how the first two women had died. Eva Taysup's corpse, on the other hand, was much more complete. Consequently, as Terry Hinz warned the court, Dr. Walker's slides were far more gruesome and disturbing. He continued with the slide presentation.

"I'll direct your attention to this black mass underneath the upper left side of the chest," Dr. Walker continued, as if he were addressing a first-year biology class. "It is some decaying organ, unidentifiable; it was decomposed. It had an active fauna, meaning it had active insects still in it—another indicator of a very short elapsed time since death."

Hinz kept the professor on course, skilfully leading him in the direction the prosecutor knew would elicit the most compelling evidence. Walker turned to the more grisly features of Eva's corpse. He pointed to a fracture line on the right side of the face and told the jury that Eva Taysup's jaw had been broken peri-mortem, meaning she had suffered the injury either immediately before or soon after death. The force of the blow had been extreme. No healing had begun. Further evidence of physical trauma included a broken rib, evident at the autopsy by looking at the ribs from the inside. The damage, Walker concluded, was the result of a compressive force to the left side of the chest.

The evidence became more chilling as every detail of Eva Taysup's suffering and murder was exposed. The left arm had been sawed at the tip of the elbow, at the funny bone. Walker gave an impromptu anatomy course to illustrate precisely how he knew the arm had been sawed, rather than smashed or chewed. From the pattern of the cut, it was apparent that the arm had been severed while fully extended. Whoever had performed this final indignity had done it very deliberately, and likely after death.

After a fifteen-minute break, Mark Brayford stood to begin his cross-examination. It is the type of questioning defence lawyers dread. Walker was intelligent and articulate, and his credentials were unimpeachable. Perhaps because of that, Brayford opened with a red herring, trying to throw the witness off guard.

"There's no dispute about the identity of the human remains," he said. "But there are a couple of things that you might assist us with. Would it be fair to say that the significance, if any, of the fact that the tobacco offerings and the human remains were in reasonably close proximity is unknown?" He was referring to the offerings and other signs of traditional aboriginal ceremonies that had been observed near the crime scenes. "There may or may not be any significance?"

"Correct," Dr. Walker replied.

Brayford plodded on, questioning the witness about the injuries to Taysup's jaw and rib. The professor conceded that they could have occurred unintentionally if someone had, as

Brayford suggested, slammed a trunk lid on her face or kicked her while she was lying on the ground. When Brayford suggested that the severed arm could have been the result of gnawing by porcupines or beaver, however, Walker conceded nothing. Rodents, he said, have chisel-like incisors that leave longitudinal grooves. "This"—he indicated the cut to Taysup's arm—"is absolutely not from chewing."

Brayford turned to more familiar ground, quizzing Walker about the media presence at the crime scene.

"RCMP officers told me that they were there," Walker replied. "I was rather busy at the time, as you might expect, but I certainly didn't see them arrive, or didn't go out to greet them."

Like the witnesses who had preceded him in, Walker was adamant that the media had not been close enough to see the murder scenes clearly, and he bristled as the defence lawyer persisted.

"How close was the media? Did they go right up to the police tape?"

"Absolutely not. They were fifty metres from the tape."

Brayford smiled. "This is a sensitive area, is it?"

"In what way, Sir?"

"Is this something that's been discussed with you by anyone, by the police?"

"Absolutely not."

"Or anyone else?"

"Absolutely not."

"So the issue of the relative proximity of the media has not been an issue raised with you by anyone?"

"You asked me at the preliminary hearing if I had talked to the media," Walker reminded him.

At the preliminary hearing, Walker had responded to Brayford's question, "Did you tell the media your name, rank, serial number, and that's it?" with a curt "I didn't even give them that." He did concede, however, that he had attended a media conference along with the RCMP and answered some reporters' questions at that time.

On re-examination, Terry Hinz floated a final question at Dr. Walker: "To come directly to the point on this, Dr. Walker, in terms of this [news conference] that you attended, brought up by my learned friend, did you or any member of the RCMP at that session indicate to the media that the third body was found wrapped in a blanket bound with electrical cord?"

"Absolutely not."

The holdback evidence was secure.

Day three of the trial opened with a defence application to scuttle the prosecution's plan to provide the jury with transcripts of the taped conversations between Crawford and Bill Corrigan. Hugh Harradence stated the case for the defence. Despite the best efforts of the RCMP stenographer and Constable Al Keller, who had proofread the transcripts while listening to the tapes, the transcripts were, nonetheless, interpretations, or opinions, of what was on the actual tapes. And that, Harradence maintained, "goes to the very crux of the argument. If the jury has a transcript, the tendency is to rely on the written word as opposed to their own interpretation of the evidence."

Mr. Justice Wright appeared to give the defence an opening. "When I hear you use the word 'interpret,' and perhaps I err, I get the sense that you're not comfortable with the form which the transcript takes with respect to some parts, at least, of the conversations."

Harradence was quick to agree. "My concern is that the jury place their own interpretation on the voices, the tone of voice that's used, the actual words that are used, the context in which they're used in, the background noise."

Wright offered to make it clear in his charge to the members of the jury that the tapes were to have priority—that they were not to rely on the transcripts alone.

"I appreciate the court's position," Harradence pushed on, "but we don't need the transcripts here. The transcripts are simply going to clutter up what otherwise will be a simple process of listening to the tapes and forming their own interpretation."

Rather than confuse the issue, Hinz retorted, the transcripts would allow the jury to identify the speakers. Otherwise, Constable Al Keller, who would be on the stand to play the tapes, would constantly be called on to stop the tapes and tell the jury who was speaking.

The judge ruled in the Crown's favour. The jury would be permitted to use the transcripts, but Wright didn't wait for his charge to instruct the jury on their use. "The transcripts can be no better than the tape," he told them, "and it's not up to somebody else to decide for you what was said or what response was made with respect to the conversations on the tape. The transcripts are intended to be an aid, something to assist you in better understanding what's on the tapes."

It was time to connect John Martin Crawford to the scientific evidence Dr. Ernie Walker had presented the previous day.

Terry Hinz called Constable Al Keller to the stand. In many ways this had become Keller's case. It was Keller who had been handed the report of a missing woman ("Angie") when he was first transferred to the General Investigation Section in 1994. It was Keller who was called on to locate Bill Corrigan when the first remains were found in early October, and, as the investigation progressed, to convince Corrigan to help the police build their case. It was Keller who went to Winnipeg to find Corrigan and extract a statement that would implicate their suspect. It was Keller who largely organized the clandestine taping of Crawford. And when the cops were certain they had a case, it was Al Keller who clamped the handcuffs on the suspected murderer.

The tape-recorded conversations between Crawford and Corrigan were essential to the Crown's case. It was only logical, then, that it was Al Keller who would introduce this vital evidence to the jury. Ernie Walker's presentation had been shocking. Keller's was equally graphic. The sound quality was excellent. If the jury had any doubts about what they were hearing, they had the transcripts in their hands.

Crawford showed up at around six o'clock and parked his mother's Cougar in front of room 165, at the rear of the Imperial 400 Motel. Corrigan let him in and the two men engaged in small talk before ordering food. An undercover RCMP officer delivered fried chicken. Corrigan encouraged Crawford to talk about the murders, which he did, crudely and graphically.

As Keller advanced the tape to the second night, John Crawford shifted his weight nervously on his bench in the prisoner's box. Once again, it was Corrigan who initiated the conversation.

"That blanket wasn't taken from the Albany, was it?"

"No."

"Hope not, 'cause that'll come right back."

With Corrigan leading him on, Crawford talked about the Shelley Napope murder.

"I was supposed to go back there and knock her teeth out. I never did that."

He left the hotel room before nine o'clock that night in order to meet his mother's strict curfew.

On the third night, with a copy of that day's *StarPhoenix* in the room featuring a story on the identification of Calinda Waterhen, Crawford told the highly excitable Corrigan not to worry. "I'll take the blame. Don't you worry. Just keep your mouth shut."

"Why did you kill them, John?"

"They made me mad."

The impact on the jury was noticeable. Crawford remained hunched over in the box.

"Why did you go back to that fucking place where you left them?"

"It was the safest place to put them," Crawford replied.

"This one here," Crawford continued. "Eva. You know that cement place at P and 11th? That's where it happened. She was going to yell rape. I said no, I paid you. She said, not enough."

He pointed to Calinda Waterhen's photo.

"This one here I did at the bushes. We were sniffing. I hit her over the head."

Keller stopped the tapes, and the newspaper that had been left in the room was entered as evidence. Hinz then invited the defence to cross-examine.

The tapes were a tough act to follow. When he rose to cross-examine, therefore, Hugh Harradence hoped to focus the jury's attention on anything but the evidence they had just heard. He began by asking Constable Keller to recall the days leading up to the initial contact with Bill Corrigan and the arrangements that were made to return Corrigan to Saskatoon. He was clearly setting the stage to discredit the reliability and motives of the Crown's key witness, Bill Corrigan.

Corrigan had signed a letter of acknowledgement with the RCMP, Keller testified. He agreed to co-operate with the investigators. In return, he would be paid $15,000 plus expenses.

"I understand Mr. Corrigan has charges outstanding in Saskatchewan?" Harradence probed.

"Those charges have been dealt with."

"What does that mean, Sir?"

"They were withdrawn this morning."

Corrigan had been charged by Saskatoon police with stealing from the Albany Hotel. The RCMP knew of the charges but did not pursue the matter. When Corrigan received his final payment of $3,750, he made restitution to the hotel and the charges were dropped.

Harradence, perhaps hoping to plant some seeds of doubt in the minds of the jury, briefly addressed Keller's role in proofing the transcripts that had been typed by a civilian employee of the RCMP. Were the transcripts accurate? Had they heard the tapes correctly? Clearly, though, the jury could judge that as well as Keller, having heard the tapes and read the transcripts themselves. Harradence concluded his cross-examination but reserved the right to recall Keller.

Mr. Justice Wright excused the jury for the day.

The appearance of Bill Corrigan, eagerly anticipated, promised to be the highlight of the trial. An inept career criminal, William James Corrigan was being encouraged to do the right thing. Perhaps for the first time in his life, he was being paid to do the right thing. Hinz knew he was a questionable witness, but he was determined to get all he could out of him before Corrigan had to face Mark Brayford's blistering cross-examination.

At 10:20 on a beautiful sunny morning, Corrigan obviously wished he could have been anywhere else but on the witness stand, in full view of a room full of lawyers, journalists, jurors, and angry members of the victims' families. The presence of

John Martin Crawford, his one-time friend, unnerved him. Corrigan gave Terry Hinz his undivided attention as the prosecutor began the examination of his star witness.

"Bill, you have a fairly long criminal record?"

"Yes, I do."

Brayford would no doubt expand on that, but at least it had been acknowledged by the Crown first.

"When I refer to an individual by the name of John Crawford," Hinz continued, "is that an individual you see present in this courtroom today?"

"Yes, right over there." Corrigan pointed. "He's trying to hide his head."

Crawford smiled nervously, but continued to slouch in his chair.

Bill Corrigan told the court about Crawford's routine, how they would cruise up 20th Street to Avenue O, then down 21st Street, looking for women. Native women, mostly. The strategy was straightforward. Crawford would pick up a girl and take her to a dark area about ten blocks from the hooker stroll. The two men and the woman would down a few beers, then Corrigan would leave the car and Crawford and the woman would have sex. Sometimes it was for money, but occasionally it was free, or so Corrigan believed. He added that he, Corrigan, did not partake in the sexual activities.

With the background in place, Hinz moved on to specifics. He asked Corrigan about the night he and Crawford had picked up Shelley Napope, the girl they both knew as Angie. Corrigan testified that Crawford had driven southwest of Saskatoon, down a gravel road that led to a grove not far from the river. The three of them drank beer until Corrigan got out of the vehicle and went for a walk. Still in view of the car, he watched as Crawford began choking the girl, then punching her. He heard the girl scream, and then he could tell that she and Crawford were having intercourse.

"I just continued to smoke my cigarette, turned around, faced the other way," Corrigan said, his voice barely audible. After ten or fifteen minutes, he says he returned to the car to find Shelley naked, crying, and dabbing at a bleeding lip.

"She wanted to go home and told John that she wasn't going

to press charges against him for rape. He told her to shut the fuck up." Corrigan said Crawford then ordered Shelley out of the car and took her into the bushes. She begged Corrigan to do something, but John said something like, "Bill isn't going to get involved." And Corrigan didn't. He remained in the car, smoking and drinking a beer.

"At one time," Corrigan went on, "it looked like he had punched her in the stomach, because she was bent over. He seemed to be more or less lifting her, kind of dragging her in further. I heard her scream."

At that point Corrigan got out of the car and walked toward Crawford and Shelley. "I saw John with a knife in his hand. She was laying on the ground, flat on her back. She was bleeding."

Corrigan was in tears. Judge Wright ordered a twenty-minute recess.

"Crawford was holding a knife," Corrigan continued when court reconvened, "about four to six inches from Angie's body. She wasn't moving. I asked John what he had done. He said, 'I killed her. She's dead. Help me. Get some branches. Help me cover her up.'"

Close to tears again, Corrigan said that he agreed to help, at least partly because Crawford was still holding the knife. Shelley's clothes were on the floor in the back of the car as the two men returned to the city.

"Johnny got out, bundled up all the clothing, running shoes and stuff, and put them all in a dumpster." Then he drove to his mother's house, where Corrigan waited in the dining room while John removed his bloodstained clothes and showered. "He called me downstairs. He was in the bathroom and he had my knife over the sink and was pouring mouthwash on the blade. He told me he was going to throw my knife into the river. I didn't want it."

The next day, Crawford called him at the Albany Hotel. They discussed the killing. "I asked him if he realized what he had done. He just kind of laughed. Said not to worry."

One night Corrigan was invited to the Crawford home for supper. While John was preoccupied with taping a movie, Bill brought in a load of groceries from Victoria Crawford's car. In the process, he discovered a bag of women's clothing. He says he questioned Crawford about the clothing.

"He told me not to worry about it because he was going to get rid of it. I think he said, 'One more doesn't matter.' He made some wisecrack that he'd get the same twenty-five years or something like that."

Corrigan was reluctant to break off the friendship, he said, because he was afraid John would think he was up to something. But over the next few weeks, he saw less and less of John Crawford.

Hinz wrapped up his examination with a few questions about Corrigan's role in taping his and Crawford's conversations. Then the judge dismissed the jury in order to address the issue of similar-fact evidence.

In order to obtain first-degree murder convictions, the Crown would have to prove that certain factors were present during the commission of the crimes: there must be an element of planning and deliberation, sexual assault, or unlawful confinement. Hinz acknowledged that there was no evidence of planning or deliberation in Crawford's actions, and only in the case of Shelley Napope was there much chance of convincing the jury that sexual assault had taken place; as there were no eyewitnesses to the killings of Calinda Waterhen and Eva Taysup no one could say with certainty what had occurred before their deaths. By introducing similar-fact evidence, however, Hinz hoped to convince the jury that Crawford's *modus operandi* invariably included sexual attacks on his victims.

There were two stories he was anxious to get before the jury. The first was the case of Louise Alice LeMay, who had gone to the police after Crawford's arrest in January 1995. The second was the case of Melanie Fiddler, who had also come forward following Crawford's arrest. Both women had been choked and raped, and threatened with worse. Hinz pointed out the common features of each attack: first, the victims were aboriginal females; second, they were picked up on the street; third, they were attacked for the purposes of forced sex. Taken as a whole, the case of John Martin Crawford fit the classical pattern of similar-fact cases. And modern law, Hinz pointed out, grants the judge broad discretion to admit such evidence if he is satisfied that its probative value is greater than its prejudicial effect.

Further, Hinz argued, in a 1990 ruling, the Supreme Court of Canada had determined that similar-fact evidence was admissible to establish the credibility of a key witness. Bill Corrigan, he conceded, "isn't exactly Citizen of the Year," but allowing the similar-fact evidence involving Fiddler and LeMay would assist the jury in deciding on his credibility.

Hugh Harradence, presenting the defence's position, provided the court with texts from *The Law of Evidence in Canada* by Mr. Justice Sopinka, commenting on the decision Hinz had referred to as well as other cases dealing with similar-fact evidence. The Supreme Court, Sopinka argued, may have appeared to relax the application of the rule in certain circumstances, but "the case should not be seen as a renunciation of the principles developed in the previous jurisprudence of the court." Not only that, but a judge "is bound to exclude evidence whose prejudicial effect outweighs its probative value. And from this perspective any discretion on the part of the judge would be limited or nonexistent."

There were glaring differences in the stories related by Melanie Fiddler and Louise LeMay, Harradence argued, and in what the Crown was alleging John Martin Crawford had visited on Calinda Waterhen, Eva Taysup, and Shelley Napope. The greatest difference, of course, was that the accused had stopped short of doing serious bodily harm to either Fiddler or LeMay.

It was Friday afternoon, and Mr. Justice Wright decided to take the weekend to consider the submissions from Hinz and Harradence.

This conclusion to the week's proceedings appeared to come as a relief to John Crawford. His eyes were heavy as he raised his arms toward a provost officer who placed handcuffs on his wrists. Victoria Crawford reached out to her son.

"I love you," she whispered, hugging him briefly.

"I love you, too," he replied, looking down at the tiny woman.

Chapter Fifteen

GUILTY

"There is a kind of ferocity in these actions that reminds me of a wild animal, a predator."

—Mr. Justice David Wright

Summer had arrived by the time the murder trial of John Martin Crawford reconvened on Monday morning, May 27. Spectators and journalists alike came to court in short-sleeved shirts and blouses as the staff fretted about the capability of the air conditioning system to keep the courtroom comfortable.

Before calling the jury, Mr. Justice Wright dealt with the similar-fact application from the Crown. It didn't take long. He noted that the issue had been widely debated in Canada and that the Supreme Court had revisited the questions on several occasions. Wright had reviewed the transcripts of the preliminary hearing in which LeMay had testified, and read Melanie Fiddler's statement to the police. He recognized similarities between their cases and the "conduct attributed to the accused" by Bill Corrigan, whom he referred to as the police agent. But there were also important differences.

"I'm obliged to look at the important and balancing questions of possible prejudice to the accused," he said. "The cases, when looked at together and sequentially, make it crystal clear that where the risk of prejudice is great and the probative value of the similar-fact evidence is not overpoweringly compelling, the evidence should not be admitted. The evidence the Crown proposed to call would, I conclude, be extremely prejudicial to the accused."

The jury, then, would not hear of John Martin Crawford's attacks on Melanie Fiddler and Louise Alice LeMay.

As courtroom theatre goes, Mark Brayford's cross-examination of William Corrigan was as good as it gets. Brayford, who is among the élite of the Saskatchewan legal community, is best known perhaps for his defence of Robert Latimer, the Wilkie-area farmer who killed his daughter to end her suffering. Consequently, Brayford now turns heads not just in Saskatoon but also across Canada. Handsome, self-assured, with curls of greying hair flowing down his back, Brayford can often be spotted driving around Saskatoon in his brown Jeep Grand Wagoneer or his bright red Porsche. Weekends he spends at Waskesiu, some 230 kilometres north of Saskatoon, hair tied back in a pony-tail, cruising in his black 1969 Cadillac Fleetwood convertible. This public version of Mark Brayford, however, bears only a slight resemblance to the real man.

Brayford is essentially a private man. Never married, but the doting father of a three-year-old daughter, he rarely discusses his personal life. His long hair inspired the satirical *Frank* magazine to dub him Jimmy Page, after the legendary Led Zeppelin guitarist. But unlike most rock stars, Brayford never touches drugs, and he drinks only moderately. He plays recreational hockey, frequently rides his bicycle in the summer, and watches his diet carefully.

He somehow manages to guard his personal privacy while

maintaining a high profile in the public eye. He frequently appears on open-line radio shows. He lectures at the University of Saskatchewan. He has played leadership roles in organizations such as the Canadian Bar Association and the Canadian Council of Criminal Defence Lawyers. Yet he recoiled in alarm when he learned that a group of friends was planning to make an occasion of a recent significant birthday at one of the legal community's favourite spots, John's Prime Rib restaurant in downtown Saskatoon.

"If there is any fuss," Brayford is reported to have warned the owner, "I'll never set foot in this place again."

The celebration was very low-key.

In court, Brayford is nothing like most of the lawyers he considers his mentors and friends. Whereas Clyne Harradence, Hugh's father, is sarcastic and animated in cross-examination, and Silas Halyk is deeply intimidating to a cowering witness, his powerful voice resonating through the courtroom, Brayford is subdued, respectful, co-operative, slow to anger, and highly effective. He comes to court prepared to do battle. He despises informants and snitches—rats, he calls them—and refuses to represent clients who are tempted to play Judas in hopes of landing a lesser sentence.

Bill Corrigan was the epitome of everything Mark Brayford despised in a Crown witness. At their first meeting, at the 1995 preliminary hearing, he had not been able to conceal his disdain for the rat recruited by the RCMP to trap John Crawford. Corrigan was a liar, a thief, and quite possibly a killer. At the very least, Brayford was going to make him earn his $15,000.

Corrigan shifted nervously in the witness box, cocking his head to one side and doing his best to look defiant and calm at the same time. It was going to be a long morning.

Terry Hinz had touched on Corrigan's criminal record. Mark Brayford was going to expose every nasty detail. The forty-four-year-old Corrigan, the jury learned, had been in trouble since he was seventeen. His first adult conviction had been in 1968 for auto theft and escaping custody, which earned him a nine-month jail sentence. To that he added other convictions. By 1974, when he started serving a ten-year sentence for armed robbery and other offences, the list had become quite sizable. Four years later, he was picked up in Brandon, Manitoba, for being unlawfully at large. Even in prison, Corrigan couldn't keep out of trouble. In 1978, three months were added to his sentence for sending a threatening letter. In 1982, in Windsor, Ontario, he earned another five years after he was convicted of wounding with intent. Corrigan had not spent a full year out of jail in the past twenty. His most recent conviction was in October 1993, a three-month sentence for fraud. Since then he had managed to stay out of trouble—or at least, he hadn't found himself facing criminal charges. But Brayford was not entirely convinced that Corrigan had been squeaky clean for that period. After leaving Saskatoon with the cash receipts from his employers at the Albany Hotel, Corrigan had moved to Winnipeg, where he set up housekeeping with a Native woman who had serious medical problems, including epilepsy. The couple lived on the woman's pension, which she qualified for as the daughter of a war hero; her father had been a highly decorated veteran of the Second World War. As for Corrigan, he did occasional work as a school crossing guard and delivered the Winnipeg *Sun*.

Mike Robinson, the private detective Brayford had hired to dig up dirt on Bill Corrigan, came back from three days in Winnipeg with information that would only add to the defence's contention that the informant was a despicable character. From Robinson, Brayford also learned some interesting information about Corrigan's whereabouts in October 1994, the month that the bodies of Eva Taysup, Calinda Waterhen, Shelley Napope, and Janet Sylvestre turned up. Apparently Corrigan didn't show up for his duties as a crossing guard on October 12, 1994. Nor had he delivered his papers on October 10, 11, or 12.

The normally patient Hinz was on his feet, wanting to know if dereliction of duty on the part of a paper carrier was a criminal offence.

"He's giving me a pain," Corrigan chirped in, emboldened by Hinz's objection.

"I've allowed you some latitude," Judge Wright told Brayford.

"But how is this material to whether he delivered the papers or not?"

"What's material, My Lord, is that there is great significance to the date of October 12, 1994. What's important is his whereabouts on that date. I think it will become apparent."

Brayford was permitted to continue. He turned to Corrigan. "You know what the significance of October the 12th, 1994, is, don't you?"

"Now that you've pointed it out, yes," said Corrigan. "If you would have asked me that in the first question I would have been able to answer it right. But you didn't."

"What happened on October 12, 1994?"

"If I'm not mistaken, I was brought here to Saskatoon."

"Someone died on that day in Saskatoon, didn't they?"

"Now that you mention it, I think I know who you're talking about, yes."

"Her name is Janet Sylvestre, right?"

"Are you talking about the young lady that was found out by the airport, so I know what I'm talking about here?"

Sylvestre had not been found anywhere near the airport, but in a grove of trees directly west of Saskatoon. Newspaper and other media reports had pinned down the location, and there was no mention of the airport, which is in the north end, albeit in the western half of the city. Why had Corrigan referred to the airport? Brayford had a theory. Only a person who had taken that route west out of Saskatoon would say that Janet Sylvestre had been found "out by the airport." It was Brayford's belief that whoever killed her had driven about the countryside west of Saskatoon and likely passed the lights of the international airport at some point. Was Corrigan present for a drive in the country that night? Why else would he refer to the airport?

"I heard it through the grapevine, or something like that," Corrigan replied unconvincingly.

Brayford let it drop. "In the penitentiary there are certain codes and rules that you must live by if you want to stay alive, correct?"

"Correct."

"And if you sell someone else out to the authorities by giving information in relation to someone, particularly if it's for favour or money, that violates the code, doesn't it?"

"Inside the penitentiary, yes."

"And the term that is used when someone gives information to the authorities and is not a good neighbour reporting criminal activity is called ratting somebody out, isn't it?"

"Yeah."

"And they refer to some person that gives information to the authorities as a rat?"

"That, or a stool pigeon. One of the two."

"It really doesn't matter to the persons inside the penitentiary. They don't draw any distinction about where someone rats someone out. It's still considered a violation of the code if you sell somebody out?"

Corrigan was anticipating Brayford's strategy. "Wrong."

"Well, you wouldn't want to go to a penitentiary and have people at the penitentiary know that you were selling out people's alleged criminal activities and acting as an informant for money, would you?"

"Wrong again."

"You'd like to go to a penitentiary and be known as an informant?"

Corrigan took a deep breath. "On this case alone I have talked to other inmates, as you put it, ex-cons, and I know where you're leading up to on this because you asked me before and you didn't give me a chance to answer. As far as the inmates inside and the ones that I know on the street and the street people, they don't classify me as a stool pigeon on this case at all. I've been told to go for it, so that's what I'm doing."

Brayford wasn't impressed. "Before this case, you were already a rat. You were selling information that had nothing to do with this case. You were already an informant, correct?"

"I'll say okay to that just to make you happy," Corrigan replied.

The remark drew a few chuckles from the gallery.

"The consequences for violating the code are usually severe beatings, or in some cases death," Brayford pressed. "Given your involvement prior to this case as an informant, it would be a very dangerous place for you to end up right now, in the penitentiary?"

"I'd say yes and no."

Now that he had shown Corrigan to be a career criminal, a rat, and an unreliable paperboy, among other things, Brayford was determined to show the jury how untruthful he was. He brought out the tale of the mythical John Potter, as well as Corrigan's four separate versions of how his buck knife had come into the possession of John Crawford. In one version, he had given the knife to Crawford at the murder scene. In another, Crawford had taken the knife from his hotel room two days before the murder. A third version had him giving the knife to Crawford in the hotel lobby. Most recently, under questioning from Terry Hinz, Corrigan had given the knife to John outside the car, moments before he used it to kill Shelley Napope.

"The reason you lied about this knife is that you don't want to be charged with murder, do you?" Brayford demanded.

"I was having alcohol problems and I was under heavy medication and I got mixed up sometimes," Corrigan replied lamely.

That he was a liar, and not a very good one, was proven.

"Mr. Corrigan, you have a two-and-a-half-year gap in your criminal record. During that period you did commit criminal offences, though, didn't you? At least, one criminal offence that's come to the attention of the authorities. On or about May the 1st of 1994 you stole $1,600 or more from the Albany Hotel. Is that correct?"

"I was accused of it," Corrigan responded, "but I was never convicted of it."

"At times did you brag that you had actually stolen $3,500 from them?"

"Not to my recollection."

"Are you denying that you fled Saskatoon with $1,600 of the hotel's money?"

"No."

"And these people hadn't done anything to you that deserved getting even with them somehow. In fact, they had helped you when you were kind of down and out, hadn't they?"

Corrigan couldn't disagree. But he could certainly squirm.

"When you were paid to give information against John Crawford, you eventually signed over sufficient money to pay $1,680 to the Albany Hotel. That isn't something you did promptly. It only happened recently that they got their money, is that right?"

"I'd say yes," Corrigan conceded.

"You were charged with theft, and a warrant was issued for your arrest. And from May the 1st, 1994, until May the 1st, 1996, you have not had that warrant executed against you, have you?"

"No."

"And if you were to be convicted of a theft, given that you have thirty-six prior convictions, thirty-five of which have resulted in jail sentences, you would fully expect to go to jail, wouldn't you?"

"More than likely, yes."

"Let me get this straight," said Brayford. "$1,680 of taxpayers' money that was going to be paid to you was instead diverted to pay for a criminal offence that you committed?"

Corrigan danced around the question. But eventually he conceded that that was why the theft charge had disappeared.

Brayford moved on to the matter of Corrigan's deal with the RCMP. "You got paid $15,000 plus expenses, and you avoided a jail sentence for a totally unrelated criminal offence."

"I'd have to say you're wrong," said Corrigan. "You better check your books again."

"I don't keep books," said Brayford. "What am I wrong about?"

Corrigan had evidently forgotten about the daily expense money he had collected, which put his total earnings well over $15,000. Judge Wright explained the meaning of per diems, and Corrigan nodded his understanding.

Brayford tried again. "You got $15,000, and you avoided a jail sentence. Is that a true statement?"

"Now that you explained yourself better, yes," Corrigan replied.

"You've avoided getting a murder charge as well so far, isn't that true?"

"Yes."

For the first time in the trial, Mark Brayford raised his voice. "I put it to you that the girl [Shelley Napope] didn't get stabbed to death, she got strangled, and it was your hands that were around her neck. And the reason you were doing it was because she said she was going to charge you with rape. Isn't that correct?"

"That is wrong," Corrigan protested.

"And the only reason the knife changed hands was that your little follower, John Crawford, was there and you wanted to make sure that his hands were just as dirty as yours and so you gave him the knife. Isn't that correct?"

"That is wrong."

Brayford returned to October 12, 1994, the night Janet Sylvestre died.

"On that date, you were in Saskatoon, weren't you?"

"Not to my recollection, no. I was in Winnipeg." Corrigan had already forgotten his earlier testimony that he had been in Saskatoon on that day.

"You know where Riddlers Bar is in Saskatoon, Saskatchewan?"

"Not really," Corrigan responded.

"Think about it. It's right around the corner, just around from 20th Street on Idylwyld. You were in that bar, at about eleven o'clock. Isn't that correct?"

"How could I be in that bar if I'm not even in the province?"

"And I put it to you that at eleven o'clock you went into that bar accompanied by Janet Sylvestre."

Corrigan maintained his position, denying that he had been in the bar with Sylvestre or that he was even in the city that night.

Brayford's face flushed. "There's one real problem with the deal you cut. You didn't get immunity, did you?"

"I didn't ask for immunity or protection or anything else."

"So you'd have to be exceedingly careful that nothing you say incriminates you in a murder charge? Because there's nothing stopping them from charging you if you do."

"Correct."

"Those are all the questions I wish to ask you. Thank you."

Later, with the jury excused, Terry Hinz let it be known to the judge that he was not pleased with Brayford's aggressive cross-examination. The defence lawyer had crossed the line in accusing Corrigan of murdering Shelley Napope, and his fierce questioning of Corrigan's criminal record had upset the balance of the trial. He asked the judge to reconsider his earlier decision to forbid the introduction of similar-fact evidence.

Brayford argued that he was entitled to attack a Crown witness's character when his credibility is very much an issue. As for the connection to Janet Sylvestre, the matter was already before the jury as a result of earlier testimony. "So the extent to which Corrigan may or may not have been the perpetrator I'd suggest has a degree of relevance that they've already drawn."

Mr. Justice Wright wanted to ponder overnight the application to allow similar-fact evidence. Court was adjourned at 3:10 Monday afternoon.

Immediately afterward, Mark Brayford and Hugh Harradence met with their client and his mother in a small interview room a few feet from the courtroom. Two RCMP provost officers were posted at the door.

The situation was critical. The lawyers knew Hinz had done his usual competent job in presenting the case. Nothing had been overlooked. The taped conversations were powerful evidence. And despite his faults, Bill Corrigan's testimony was damaging. Earlier in the trial, Crawford had told Harradence he didn't want to testify. He feared Terry Hinz, and knew he wouldn't look good in front of the jury. Brayford did not want John to testify, but he needed to hear it from John himself, in front of his mother.

"We're standing in a hurricane right now, facing it. Those tapes with your words on it are deadly," Brayford told John. "So, you're quite satisfied you want to give up your right to testify?"

John replied, "Yeah, yeah, yeah."

Brayford turned to Victoria Crawford.

"Do you have anything you want to ask me at this time or say about whether John testifies?"

"Not really," said John's mother.

"You agree with John?"

"Yes, I do."

The meeting was over. John and Victoria Crawford signed a document confirming their instructions to Brayford and Harradence. John would not testify, and the defence would call no evidence. The six-paragraph authorization also stated that the Crawfords were fully satisfied with the legal services provided by Mark Brayford and Hugh Harradence.

When court reconvened on Tuesday, May 28, Mr. Justice Wright for the second time rejected the Crown prosecutor's request to allow the jury to hear the similar-fact evidence. The jury was recalled.

Mark Brayford rose and addressed the bench. "The defence elects to call no evidence, My Lord."

Like many accused murderers, John Martin Crawford would not testify, nor would he offer any evidence to counter the evidence that had been presented by the Crown. Some members of the jury appeared perplexed.

It was up to the lawyers now. Hinz and Brayford would make their final arguments based on the evidence that had been tendered. They could analyze, and they could emphasize various aspects of the evidence. But there would be no new evidence. The jury had heard it all.

Terry Hinz spoke first.

"For all the tragedy and gravity of this case," he said, "it has been a short one."

He then undertook a methodical review of the evidence.

"Bill Corrigan's primary role in this case," he continued, "was to testify about the actual circumstances of the death of Shelley Napope. His graphic and chilling account of the death of that girl speaks for itself. If you accept that evidence unquestionably, John Crawford killed that girl. That killing took place in the course of a sexual assault on her. When you murder someone while you are sexually assaulting them, that is first-degree murder. Can you accept Bill Corrigan's evidence? Or, as Mr. Brayford will suggest to you, is Bill Corrigan the killer? I suggest that the key to resolving the question of Bill Corrigan's credibility and his role in the Shelley Napope incident is to be found in the whole issue of the tape recordings."

Ask yourselves, Hinz said: if Corrigan was guilty of Shelley Napope's murder, would he have agreed to work with the police in secretly recording John Crawford's conversations? Clearly, any such conversation would bring out Corrigan's own role in the murder, and that would be the last thing in the world he would agree to do. "Bill Corrigan may be many things, but he's not out of his mind. If Bill Corrigan was guilty or felt he had anything to hide in relation to Shelley Napope's death, wouldn't you think he'd ask for immunity for that? He never asked for that."

The tapes spoke for themselves, Hinz told the jury. Even with the confusion over the name, it was clear that John had admitted to killing Shelley Napope. He had clearly admitted to the other two killings, and provided details. He had confirmed that the two bodies found near Shelley's remains were those of Eva Taysup and Calinda Waterhen.

Still hoping to obtain first-degree murder convictions on all three charges, Hinz needed the sexual assault connection.

"We know that he had sexual contact with these victims," he said, and read from the transcript: *'They found the bodies. But all the sperm and all that is gone.'* You'll note that this remark is made in connection to both of these victims. At another point Crawford says, *'She was going to yell rape. She said, 'you didn't pay me enough' and I choked her.'*

Hinz moved on to the question of the holdback evidence, reading once more from the transcript: *"'The only one I'm worried about is the one that was buried with the blanket,' Crawford said. 'I didn't have sex with her on the blanket, I just covered her up and put a cord around her. So if they find the cord they wouldn't find my fingerprints.'* Members of the jury, only the killer of Eva Taysup could know those details."

Hinz had been on his feet for just fifteen minutes.

"The guilt of an accused at a criminal trial," he concluded, "must be proved beyond a reasonable doubt. A reasonable doubt must have some foundation in the evidence. Reasonable doubts do not come about from saying, 'Maybe a UFO did it.' It's got to be something solid in the evidence. And there is nothing solid in the defence suggestion that this accused could somehow have knowledge of Eva Taysup's burial from some media source. John Crawford knew those details. That, more than anything else in the case, proves that John Crawford was the killer."

Mark Brayford opened his final argument with a short lesson in law.

"The Crown has to prove each and every element of this case. Not just that John Crawford knows what happened, heard what happened, was there, witnessed something. That doesn't make it. The Crown has to be in a position, in order to get a conviction, to prove that John Crawford committed the murder and that his knowledge wasn't gained in some other way."

The Crown in this case, he said, had a huge problem: William Corrigan. A tape recording was not a confession, and Corrigan's conversations with John Crawford could hardly be considered objective. "William Corrigan was in control of that interview and he knew my client. I suggest to you that, if you listen to William Corrigan's voice, he was nervous throughout the whole three days." Indeed, Corrigan's life depended on setting up his friend John Crawford; if he didn't do it right, his life might be in danger.

"The amount of talking that John Crawford does on the tape is minute," Brayford continued. "William Corrigan talks all the time. The reason he talks all the time is he doesn't want my client to get a word in edgewise."

As to the holdback evidence, Brayford reasoned, "This blanket issue has become something of a red herring. That was one of those things where counsel gets to have a little bit of fun. How many versions did we hear about what could or could not be seen, and who could or could not see what, from those police officers? With the greatest respect for my learned friend, I would submit to you that what the Crown's case proves as to what could or could not be seen is just not there. So we don't have a clue."

Like Terry Hinz, Mark Brayford also talked about reasonable doubt: "You can't speculate on reasonable doubt," he said, but "we shouldn't approach it from that direction." Instead, one should approach the question from the standpoint of "Has the Crown proven each element beyond a reasonable doubt? Are all the elements proven? Are you satisfied? Are all the elements

there? We can't fill in the elements of the Crown's case by speculation, by guessing, by assuming this is what happened, by
assuming that when he says something, well, this is what he
meant. And if you have a nagging doubt, if there's some troubling
aspect of the case that you don't feel sure about, then the law
requires that you do your duty."

He was very confident, he said, that the jury would find that
nagging doubt. Then he took a final shot at the Crown's star witness: "Would you want any fellow citizen to be convicted on the
evidence of William Corrigan? Is he a liar or isn't he?

"My client's fate is now in your hands. Thank you very much,
ladies and gentlemen."

The jury was excused.

Terry Hinz had decided that the first-degree charges relating to
the deaths of Eva Taysup and Calinda Waterhen weren't going to
stick. He asked the judge to withdraw them. The most serious
charge the jury would be permitted to consider would be second-degree murder. Mr. Justice Wright concurred. He had already
come to that conclusion himself.

As is customary, the two sides offered opinions as to what
points Mr. Justice Wright might want to include or emphasize in his
charge to the jury. They touched on the issues of first- and second-degree murder, and whether manslaughter might be an
available finding of guilt. Hugh Harradence suggested that the
jury should be allowed to consider the defence of drunkenness,
given Crawford's chronic abuse of alcohol, pills, and solvents
throughout 1992. In the end it would be up to Wright to outline
the jury's options.

He began his charge to the jury on Thursday, May 30, 1996, at
9:30 AM. He spoke for almost two hours, leaving no detail unat-
tended as he instructed the six women and six men on the principles of law that applied to the case against John Martin Crawford.
He began by reminding them that they alone had the responsibility for determining guilt or innocence: "You should approach
your duties objectively, that is, without any pity or sympathy for

the accused or any prejudice against him. You are to be governed solely by the evidence introduced in this case, by the exhibits that have been presented here, and by the law and absolutely nothing else."

He told them that the possible penalty or punishment should never be discussed or considered by them. That responsibility would fall entirely on the shoulders of the trial judge if a guilty verdict or verdicts were returned. "Proof beyond a reasonable doubt," Wright explained,

> has been achieved when a juror feels sure of the guilt of the accused. It is that degree of proof which convinces the mind and satisfies the conscience, so that you, as conscientious jurors, feel bound to act upon it. Conversely, when the evidence you have heard leaves you, as a responsible juror, with some lingering or nagging doubt with respect to the proof of some essential element of the offence with which the accused is charged, so you are unable to say to yourself the Crown has proven the guilt of the accused beyond a reasonable doubt, your duty then is to acquit.

Mr. Justice Wright then addressed the specifics of this case. The jury learned for the first time that the most serious charge the accused could be convicted of in the deaths of Eva Taysup and Calinda Waterhen was second-degree murder. Crawford had been indicted on three counts of first-degree murder, but "the Crown has concluded that there was insufficient evidence that the murders of Eva Taysup and Calinda Waterhen were planned and deliberate." As to the murder of Shelley Napope, while there was insufficient evidence to indicate that the action had involved planning and deliberation, the Crown was pursuing the first-degree murder charge because there was evidence that a sexual assault was alleged to have occurred at the time of the murder.

The jury could consider manslaughter in its options, the judge instructed.

There is a tiered process. We look at first-degree murder and the constituent offences or elements. If that is not established, then you turn to the issue of second-degree murder, and, on the basis of the instructions I have given you there, if that is not established, you then turn to the question of manslaughter, and, of course, if that's not established, then you must acquit.

As was his duty and prerogative, Mr. Justice Wright commented on specific evidence that had been presented during the trial. He was attempting to demonstrate to the jury the essential differences between inference and speculation. He was concerned about the defence's contention that Bill Corrigan had been in Saskatoon the night Janet Sylvestre was killed. "On the basis of the evidence I heard," he told them, "there is no evidence that Corrigan was here that night, no matter what he was doing in Winnipeg or elsewhere. In my respectful view, the suggestion that you may conclude, or assume, that Corrigan was here constitutes speculation."

As for Mark Brayford's suggestion that many of the things Crawford mentioned on the tape were based on what he had learned from various sources, that, too, was merely speculation. Wright instructed the jury to ignore the issue of immunity for Bill Corrigan and the suggestion that the media might have been able to see the holdback evidence.

Like almost everyone involved in the case, the judge's opinion of William Corrigan was not high.

I must advise you that, in accepting Corrigan's evidence, you must be very careful. It is unsafe to rely on the evidence of a person like Corrigan in isolation. Corrigan might be looked upon by the law as an accomplice with respect to the death of Shelley Napope. Corrigan supplied the knife, he helped cover up Napope's body. You may conclude that he assisted the accused or that his involvement was, as he put it, completely innocent and prompted by fear of the accused. The rule is that the evidence of an accomplice must be looked at with extreme caution and very often will require corroboration. Your responsibility is to look for other independent evidence to support his oral testimony. One such source would be the tapes. We have heard that Corrigan has a long and serious criminal record, and that a number of his convictions are for offences that involve lying and dishonesty. You must be extremely cautious about accepting his evidence because it bears significantly on his credibility, on his reliability.

There is also the fact the police paid Corrigan a substantial sum of money in return for participating in taping the interviews and testifying. And finally, one of the factors that constituted the bargain between Corrigan and the police was that the theft charge against Corrigan was withdrawn, and that was part of the package.

It was noon. The jury would begin its deliberations after lunch.

Throughout the afternoon, as reporters reclined in lawn chairs by the back door of the courthouse and family members chain-smoked on the front steps, the consensus was that this jury wouldn't need more than a few minutes to convict John Martin Crawford. This, as the lawyers say, was a slam dunk case. The man had admitted to killing three women. The police had it on tape. He was guilty as sin.

By mid-afternoon the mood had changed. The relatives of Shelley Napope huddled in the corridor, no doubt wondering what the jury could possibly be pondering after all the evidence they had seen and heard.

Patrick Asapace, a first cousin to Shelley, talked to a reporter. He admitted that he had been in prison for serious crimes, including attempted murder. He had done time in Manitoba's infamous Stony Mountain Penitentiary and at the Saskatchewan

Penitentiary in Prince Albert. He had met Bill Corrigan before, and he didn't like him. "He should be up there charged with the same offences as Crawford. Who protected these girls when they were being raped and murdered? This asshole could have."

At five o'clock there was still no word from the jury. Victoria Crawford wanted to speak to her son. Hugh Harradence was dispatched to make the arrangements. He returned a few minutes later.

"He's sleeping, Victoria. I couldn't wake him up."

John Crawford, awaiting a verdict on three murder charges, was asleep in the holding cell, probably the most relaxed person in the building.

Terry Hinz paced the hallway. His ready smile could not hide his apprehension.

Downstairs in the barristers' lounge, Mark Brayford and Hugh Harradence talked with a freelance journalist who had been following the case. Cindy Ritchie, the court clerk, dropped in for a chat. What could be keeping the jury?

A sheriff's officer announced that the jury was taking a break for supper. Everyone could relax. Television reporters, already past deadline, rushed to file reports to their respective stations.

Common wisdom has it that juries like to squeeze one more meal out of the government before returning with a verdict. They'll decide to have supper, then deliver their verdict right after dessert. It didn't happen in this case. The hours passed slowly. It was getting dark. It was becoming a distinct possibility that the jury would retire for the night without reaching a verdict.

At 10:20 PM Rex Badger, the jocular sheriff's officer assigned to supervise the jury, threw open the back door of the courthouse. "We've got a verdict," he announced.

Moments later, after the lawyers, police officers, and other spectators had been informed, court was called into session. The jury entered Courtroom No. 1 on the top floor of Queen's Bench Courthouse. Seven reporters were in the room. Two men, one of them Pat Asapace, took seats near the back. Janice Acoose, a Saskatoon educator and writer who had been present for most of the trial, found her spot on a second-row bench. Victoria

Crawford, looking anxious and tired, clutched her purse as she sat down in the second row, next to a journalist, directly behind the prisoners' box. Her eyes darted about the courtroom, finally resting on the shoulders of her son, not more than three metres away.

The court clerk rose.

"Ladies and gentlemen of the jury, have you agreed upon your verdict?"

"We have," the foreman replied.

"How say you, do you find the accused guilt or not guilty on count number one, as to second-degree murder?"

"Guilty."

"How say you, do you find the accused guilty or not guilty on count number two, as to first-degree murder?"

"Guilty."

"How say you, do you find the accused guilty or not guilty on count number three, as to second-degree murder?"

"Guilty."

John Martin Crawford didn't flinch. He was utterly expressionless. So was Victoria.

Mark Brayford asked that the jury be polled on count number two, the first-degree murder conviction for Shelley Napope. One by one the twelve jurors confirmed their guilty verdict.

The jury's work was not quite finished. The sentence for first-degree murder was automatic: life, with no parole for twenty-five years. For second-degree murder, the judge has some discretion in determining parole eligibility, from a minimum of ten years to a maximum of twenty-five. Under the Criminal Code, however, judges must ask the jury if they have any recommendations on the point. The jury was excused to consider it. They returned a few minutes later and reported that the jury did not wish to make any recommendation. Mr. Justice Wright excused the jury. They had done their duty.

In 1996, when John Crawford was convicted, Parliament had not yet passed legislation providing for consecutive sentences for murderers. Consequently, all three sentences Crawford received are being served concurrently. Since the sentence for first-degree murder was automatic, the effect of the other two would be minimal. Even so, Mark Brayford wanted a few moments to discuss the sentencing implications with his client. Mr. Justice Wright ordered a brief adjournment.

Victoria Crawford turned wearily to a journalist sitting next to her, her eyes heavy with fatigue. "Is it over?" she asked quietly.

"Not quite," he told her. "Mr. Brayford wants to talk to you and John."

"Oh."

Crawford didn't need much time to think about it. He wanted to deal with the sentence immediately. But Terry Hinz had other ideas.

"My Lord, I do have a few words to say on the question of the parole and eligibility period on counts one and three, somewhat academic though it might be. Mr. Crawford has a record. Of particular relevance is the fact that this is not the first time this accused has been convicted of homicide. In 1982 in Lethbridge, Alberta, he was convicted of manslaughter and sentenced to ten years imprisonment."

Hinz read from an affidavit that had been filed in support of the wiretap authorization: That John Martin Crawford was convicted of the death of Mary Jane Serloin, that the body of Mary Jane Serloin was located in a back alley in a downtown area in the City of Lethbridge, that Mary Jane Serloin was Native in racial origin and was left nude, laying on her back, the body showed signs of beating and visible human bite marks.

Hinz was arguing for the harshest possible sentence for the second-degree murder convictions, although they would, of course, be served concurrently with the mandatory first-degree sentence. It complicated matters. Mark Brayford rose to address the matter.

Looking ahead fifteen years, he said, his client might wish to seek early parole based on what is generally termed Canada's "faint hope clause," whereby convicted murderers can apply to the courts for early parole after they have served fifteen years of a life sentence. Brayford was well aware that the controversial provision might not exist in another fifteen years, but he wanted to be sure that a potential jury at that time would not have an unreasonably prejudicial view of John Martin Crawford.

"I'm not suggesting that parole is ever even a likelihood in my client's case," he argued, "but we don't know what the future holds. This was a period of time, in 1992, when my client was heavily involved in not just alcohol and drug abuse, but in solvent abuse as well. Throughout that period, his mother, who has stood valiantly by him, tried desperately to deal with his problem and had him in and out of about eight treatment institutions."

In the future, a parole board might feel that whatever had motivated John Crawford's behaviour might have been dealt with. Brayford therefore urged Judge Wright to let the first-degree sentence carry the way and set parole eligibility for the two counts of second-degree murder at fifteen years each.

It was after 11:00 PM.

Sentencing was adjourned until the next day.

At precisely two o'clock that Friday afternoon, Mr. Justice David Wright entered Courtroom No. 1 and began his remarks. He delivered a scathing condemnation of thirty-four-year-old John Martin Crawford, who was seated directly in front of him. It took less than five minutes.

"I begin," he said, "by observing that in the latter stages of this trial the victims seemed to have been largely forgotten. I don't suggest that that was due to callousness on the part of anyone, but in my observation, that's what happened."

Most observers hadn't noticed, but while the focus was on John Crawford, the lawyers, the police investigators, and particularly on the Crown's star witness, the perfidious Bill Corrigan, erstwhile friend of the accused, nary a word was spoken about Eva Taysup, Calinda Waterhen, and Shelley Napope. They would be referred to variously as "the victims," "the deceased," "the remains," or "skeletons," and occasionally, as "the three women."

Judge Wright continued: "These were three young women of Native ancestry who happened to be prostitutes. They had families, friends, and lives, although perhaps not very good lives, but they made decisions for themselves. They lived as they wished, although in many cases, I suspect, as necessity dictated, but they were lives.

"What was there about these four victims," asked Judge Wright, including Mary Jane Serloin in his remarks,

> that made Mr. Crawford feel that he could take their lives after sexually assaulting them, confining them, terrorizing them, and then brutally killing them?
>
> And finally, what on earth can explain his actions in mutilating two of them? I refer to his conviction with respect to Ms. Serloin. She was left naked, the final indignity, on her back and exposed and mutilated by biting. Ms. Taysup's arm was cut off at the elbow, for what possible reason?
>
> It appears to me that Mr. Crawford was attracted to his victims for four reasons: one, they were young; second they were women; third, they were Native; and fourth, they were prostitutes. They were persons separated from the community and their families. The accused treated them with contempt, brutality; he terrorized them, he violated them sexually, he confined them, and ultimately he killed them. He seemed determined to destroy every vestige of their humanity. He left three of them naked and lying on the ground. There is a kind of ferocity in these actions that reminds me of a wild animal, a predator.
>
> The accused has shown no remorse, absolutely none, no regrets, there's been no effort to explain his actions and in fact we know from the tapes that he laughed about the killings.

Mr. Justice Wright had been named to the Court of Queen's Bench on December 19, 1980. John Crawford's crimes, he said, were among the most disturbing he had encountered in those sixteen years: "These were horrifying murders. This accused should never be allowed to leave prison. I am limited by law to increasing the periods in which he is ineligible for parole to twenty-five years, and I have absolutely no hesitation in doing so. I would make it longer if I could."

He added a rider to his sentence: "I am instructing the clerk to endorse on each of the Warrants of Committal, an endorsement directing the attention of the National Parole Board to the comments I have made here, and I'm also directing that a copy of my decision be entered in the court file."

A handful of reporters and family members were present when the trial of John Martin Crawford came to an end. One of them was Bev Taysup, Eva's sister. "This doesn't make me feel any better," she said. "It doesn't take away the hurt or the emptiness."

Chapter Sixteen

THE APPEAL

"I explained to her that John was not a North American football hero, that we had no race card to play, that John had a previous conviction for manslaughter . . ."

— Mark Brayford

Like any good defence attorney, Mark Brayford is prepared to represent an accused person regardless of how disturbing the charges may be against him or her. Even cases in which the Crown has what appears to be an airtight case and the outcome is a foregone conclusion, he believes, are worthy of a vigorous defence. But appeals are a different matter. Brayford will not initiate an appeal if he does not feel there is sufficient legal merit.

In the days following Crawford's convictions, the matter of an appeal was discussed with Crawford and his mother, Victoria. John, looking at a life in prison with virtually no hope of being paroled, was a realist. He wanted no part of an appeal.

His mother, however, insisted that every possible effort be made to prove her son's innocence. She pressed Brayford to quote her a fee for handling the appeal. When he gave her a deliberately outrageous figure, she barely flinched. At that point, he told her firmly that he was not about to attempt an appeal he felt had no legal foundation, and he resigned as John Crawford's attorney.

Victoria refused to give up, though, and on June 27, 1996, barely within the thirty-day limit, Bob Hrycan, a partner in the Regina firm of Shumiatcher Hrycan, delivered a Notice of Appeal to the registrar at the Saskatchewan Court of Appeal in Regina. The original Notice of Appeal contained six grounds, dealing mainly with the admissibility of the wiretap evidence that had been so damaging at the trial. As with all Notices of Appeal, however, this one left the door open for counsel to amend it before it actually reached the court. By the spring of 1998, after numerous delays and adjournments, the focus of the appeal had indeed been narrowed. Victoria's lawyer was prepared to argue that John Martin Crawford had not had a competent and adequate defence from his lawyers, lead counsel Mark Brayford and co-counsel Hugh Harradence.

Mark Brayford was, understandably, livid. Hugh Harradence was only slightly less outraged. Questioning the ability and the integrity of two of Saskatchewan's most highly regarded lawyers was an unusual basis for an appeal, to say the least. For the next six months, Brayford and Harradence engaged in a battle of words with Hrycan as they were forced to defend their defence of John Martin Crawford.

On June 11, 1998, Mark Brayford opened a three-page letter to Bob Hrycan with this admonishment: "You have an ethical obligation not to mislead the Court, and to ensure that the Court fairly has all the facts." The appeal would criticize Brayford and Harradence for not putting John Crawford and a psychiatrist on the stand in the hope of achieving a lesser conviction of manslaughter on the basis of diminished capacity and to challenge the testimony of the Crown's key witness, Bill Corrigan. Brayford's tone was barely civil:

It is totally improper for you to argue this when you and John Crawford both know that at the time of the trial, John Crawford was adamantly denying that he choked those two girls [Eva Taysup and Calinda Waterhen] to death. Hugh Harradence and I could not therefore advance manslaughter at the trial on the basis you suggest because John Crawford's position at trial was that his confession to William Corrigan was false. John Crawford was telling us that he did not kill those women.

You know those were John's instructions to us at the time of the trial because I discussed this extensively with you at the commencement of the appeal process, which was before you prepared the Amended Notice of Appeal.

John Crawford was claiming his innocence to us, Victoria Crawford was claiming his innocence, and obviously under those circumstances, we could not put forward the defence you are criticizing us for not advancing.

It is totally improper for you to mislead the Court into believing we had that option and I request that you and John Crawford make the Court aware of this letter and the complete contents of that taped meeting between John Crawford, Victoria Crawford, Hugh Harradence, and myself.

The issue at the tape-recorded meeting was whether or not John should take the stand in his own defence.

Brayford claimed that John had freely chosen not to take the stand and that the affidavit Hrycan referred to his two-page version of the dialogue and had entered as an exhibit at the appeal— as a transcript—lacked several lines of advice and comments from Brayford and Harradence.

Victoria Crawford swore that she had reviewed the transcript and believed it to be "an accurate representation of what

Mr. Brayford said and the replies of myself and John," though Brayford begged to differ. "The sworn statement of accuracy is false," he wrote.

That concluded round one. Hugh Harradence weighed in for round two. "I am dismayed," he wrote to Hrycan in June 1998, "by the manner in which I have found out about these allegations concerning me, and I certainly would have expected a greater degree of courtesy from a person holding a certificate to practise law in Saskatchewan." Harradence told Hrycan that he acted on instructions from John Crawford based on the client's contention that he was innocent of the charges.

In late summer, Hrycan sent a twenty-question letter requesting details about Brayford and Harradence's thinking in defending John Crawford. Brayford responded several weeks later:

> I am responding to your questions that seem predicated on the false premise that we had an opportunity to run a manslaughter type defence based upon diminished capacity through a combination of alcohol or psychiatric problems. As you are aware from my initial discussions with you prior to commencing this appeal, by the time of trial John Crawford was adamantly insisting he was innocent, and so the only defence we could advance was to attempt to have him found not guilty.
>
> Your questions presuppose that other avenues were available to us, which was not the case. In answering the following questions, I believe it is important that any reader understands that they are premised upon a line of defence that you know was not available to us, and hence this lengthy digression into these many irrelevant areas obscures the key point: you are criticizing us for not advancing a defence that you knew was not available to us at the time you wrote your Factum based on your conversations with me.

Furthermore, you are criticizing us for not advancing the defence of manslaughter, which defence would be unlikely to be of any benefit to Mr. Crawford.

Brayford proceeded to respond to each of Hrycan's questions, raising issues that would be re-examined at the Court of Appeal.

Proceedings in all levels in Canadian courts are generally marked by civility and exaggerated politeness. Opponents interact with one another with respect and cordiality, however forced. On Thursday, January 21, 1999, when John Martin Crawford appeared before the Saskatchewan Court of Appeal in Regina, the cordiality was more forced than usual when Bob Hrycan stood to address the three Appeal Court judges: Calvin Tallis, who had represented David Milgaard in 1969, Marjorie Gerwing, and Gary Lane. Ken MacKay represented the Crown.

The court agreed to Hrycan's request to introduce affidavits from John Crawford, Victoria Crawford, and Dr. Stanley Semrau, the Kelowna psychiatrist who had interviewed Crawford in 1998. The justices also agreed to hear *viva voce*, or oral, testimony from Mark Brayford, Hugh Harradence, and Victoria Crawford, a somewhat unusual event in the Court of Appeal.

Hrycan told the three judges that there were four issues they would be asked to consider:

- trial counsel should not have rejected lesser included verdicts as a potential benefit to the accused
- trial counsel should have had Mr. Crawford examined by a psychiatrist to determine the availability of lesser included verdicts
- trial counsel should not have proceeded to trial to obtain an acquittal when there was no prospect of doing so
- trial counsel should have advised both the appellant and Mrs. Crawford of the hopelessness of the case before undertaking the trial

Victoria Crawford, dressed in a grey pantsuit, was the first witness to take the stand. She was obviously nervous, and unsure of what was expected of her. Hrycan, knowing his witness was inarticulate and tense, carefully led her through a series of background questions, finally landing on the issue of hiring a psychiatrist to examine her son:

> *Hrycan:* Was there any discussion with the defence lawyers about a psychiatrist?
>
> *Victoria Crawford:* They told me it was too expensive. Everything was too expensive. But it was not. I paid them both all my money. I could have raised it for psychiatrists.
>
> *Hrycan:* How did you expect the psychiatrist to assist?
>
> *Victoria Crawford:* To find out why he said these things, [and] if he could stand a trial. I didn't want my son to get a nervous breakdown. Why did he say these things to Bill Corrigan in that room and stuff like that? A normal person doesn't do that.

Victoria Crawford told the Appeal Court of her disappointment that the defence lawyers had visited John only twice in jail prior to the trial. And she wondered why John hadn't been put on the witness stand to explain his actions.

Under cross-examination, Victoria Crawford was contradicted by the words of the affidavit she had sworn for the appeal. In the affidavit she acknowledged that, at one point in preparing for the trial, Mark Brayford had discussed the idea of having a psychiatrist examine John. Ken MacKay read from the document:

> The way I understood it the doctor would help to show John was crazy. I did not see why it was a good thing to show John was crazy when he was innocent. Mr. Brayford explained that a doctor could show manslaughter instead of murder.

A few minutes later, MacKay asked, "Did Mr. Brayford discuss with you whether a psychiatrist would be of benefit in having John found, at the end of the trial, not guilty of murder, but guilty of manslaughter? Did Mr. Brayford ever discuss that with you?"

Victoria Crawford replied, "No."

Mr. Justice Tallis invited Hrycan to re-examine the witness.

"Did you understand Mr. MacKay's questions?" Hrycan asked, but Victoria Crawford was given no chance to respond.

"I don't think that's a proper question to put in re-examination, Mr. Hrycan," Mr. Justice Tallis interrupted.

"I don't think I'll ask any questions," Hrycan decided.

Mark Brayford was called to the stand. He told the court about his first meeting with John Crawford soon after the RCMP had arrested him.

> I confronted him with the strength of the Crown's case and pointed out the hopelessness of it, as I saw it, based on the evidence that Mr. Hinz had explained to me. And I confirmed with Mr. Crawford that he had, in effect, confessed to the police. He had already accepted that he was going to be found guilty of these charges, in my view, and that he wasn't going to get out of jail. I reviewed with him that there's three possibilities when you kill somebody, that there's first-degree murder, second-degree murder, and manslaughter, and I was probably referring to insanity or not guilty by reason of mental incompetence as insanity and reviewed those options. And, in view of the fact that John had previously been sentenced to ten years for manslaughter— "

"My Lord," Bob Hrycan interrupted, "although this is an inappropriate time to break, I understand that, due to the appellant's medical condition, it would be advisable if the Court recessed for a period of time."

John Crawford needed to use the washroom. He appeared weaker than he had at his trial three years earlier, though he'd managed to add another thirty or forty pounds to his bulky frame. He was pale and he took short, shallow breaths.

When court was reconvened, Brayford continued his testimony.

> When we were done going through the Crown's case, I believe that Mr. Crawford recognized that it appeared futile. But no decision had been made at that point. We did discuss whether there was any point to even running a trial, or whether or not he should simply plead guilty and not waste his mother's money.

John Crawford, Brayford continued, knew full well that obtaining manslaughter convictions—either by agreement with the prosecution or by convincing a jury that the deaths were not first- or second-degree murder—would not do him any good. Fourteen years earlier he'd been convicted of manslaughter and done his time. He didn't need Brayford to explain to him that there was no way he would get anything less than life imprisonment for manslaughter, and that he would never get parole after killing three more people.

Later, Brayford testified, Crawford's position changed dramatically: "He went from simply challenging whether they could prove these allegations to eventually saying 'I'm not guilty. Those allegations aren't true.'"

Hrycan interrupted again, politely: "If I may interrupt you, why were the lesser verdicts of manslaughter, which carry no minimum for parole eligibility, excluded as of no benefit?"

Brayford smiled. It was a question he was prepared for. "As I understand it, John Crawford would be ranked the second, numerically, [next to] Clifford Olson. I mean, this is four deaths that he would have been convicted of for manslaughter. Any suggestion that you would parole a serial killer who had the chance of being released once and then gone out and re-offended . . ." He let the sentence trail off. "Even John Crawford understood how ridiculous the suggestion that he might get parole was."

As Hrycan directed questions at Brayford, the defence lawyer explained why they had not attempted to put forward a defence of insanity, and why such a hopeless case had gone to trial in the first place:

Hrycan: What did you think the appellant's chances were at trial?

Brayford: Very poor. I communicated that to him and he seemed resigned to the fact that we were going to lose and that he was going to spend the rest of his life in jail. But he still wanted to have his trial. He didn't want people to call him crazy. He didn't want to be found insane, and he wanted to take the only shot that really had a chance of him getting out of jail in his lifetime, and that was to be found not guilty.

Hrycan: How were you going to obtain an acquittal at trial for him?

Brayford: I had been telling [the Crawfords] that his chances of being found not guilty were very poor. But the fact of the matter is, if you've got a jury of twelve people, you do not know what they might do. And, I think it's fair to say that a lot of people were not expecting Mr. [O. J.] Simpson to be found not guilty in view of the DNA evidence that was being tendered against him, and yet he was. And that trial, specifically, was discussed by Mrs. Crawford.

Hrycan: And what response, if any, did you give to her when she brought that forward?

Brayford: I explained to her that John wasn't a North American football hero, that we had no race card to play, that John had a previous conviction for manslaughter that might well come out in the trial. I do not want to diminish how poor I thought his chances of winning the trial were. However, he didn't have any other options.

Bill Corrigan represented a grain of hope, in that a jury might reject the damning conversations they heard on tape because of Corrigan's lack of credibility. Brayford had chosen to concentrate much of his attention on that aspect of the Crown's case.

"You just don't know what might happen when you're dealing with an unsavoury witness," Brayford explained.

> The strength of the Crown's case against my client was the tape recording and William Corrigan. So, if they're going to be putting in the tape, they're also going to be tendering William Corrigan. The great weakness was that my client's voice is on that tape, making admissions. But, the Crown's case was tied inextricably to this very unsavoury witness who is a perjurer and who, I believed, would make a bad impression with the jury. There's always a remote chance that the jury would be distracted from the tape by William Corrigan's evidence.

Canadian juries are not permitted to discuss what went on in the jury room behind closed doors, but Brayford suggests the reason they took more than seven hours to reach their verdicts was because "they were troubled by William Corrigan. But at the end of the day they still had that tape."

There was another element of uncertainty that both the Crown and the defence team were aware of: the murder of Janet Sylvestre. Despite the official RCMP position, the circumstances were more than coincidental. And John Crawford had been charged with raping Janet in 1992.

"I don't think anybody purports to say that they really are comfortable as to what really happened out there," Brayford testified. He continued:

> There was evidence linking John Crawford to this fourth killing, and there's evidence linking a person I won't name to this fourth killing, who was a

friend of my client. And this caused a grey area as to what the real facts were. As much as there was a strong case against my client, there was this one element of uncertainty that was introduced by this fourth killing. And, in spite of significant evidence against my client, the Crown chose not to introduce that fourth killing, lest it might cause some uncertainty with respect to the other three.

Bob Hrycan's examination of Mark Brayford had not gone well for John Crawford. Brayford had no difficulty in delineating his strategy for the defence of a serial killer who had come to him with an unachievable assignment.

Mr. Justice Calvin Tallis had a few questions for Brayford.

"I don't think anybody asked you how long you have been practising law," he asked.

"I've been practising law for twenty years."

"And, during the course of your years of practice, has it primarily been in the field of criminal law?"

"Almost exclusively for at least half of the practice, and very much prior to that."

Tallis, well aware of Brayford's reputation, knew the answers to his queries before he posed them; he simply wanted Brayford's credentials on the record.

"During the course of your interviews with the appellant in this particular case," said Tallis, "did he have any difficulty in understanding the procedure and considerations that you explained to him?"

"No, he didn't, my Lord. He is a very street-smart individual. He had served a significant term in a penitentiary before I met him, and he was quite knowledgeable about the justice system. He had been involved in a homicide before, so he knew the workings of parole and why he couldn't get parole better than I did."

Hugh Harradence further defused Hrycan's arguments when he took the stand to explain why John Crawford had not been put on the stand: "During a break, John summoned me into the waiting room and said, 'I am not going to testify, that prosecutor will tear me to shreds.' I said to John, 'We'll discuss that later, after the Crown closes its case.'"

When it was decided that John would not testify, as we have seen, Harradence prepared an authorization in which John stated that it was his wish not to testify. Both John Crawford and Victoria Crawford signed it. The brief document also contained the sentence: "I am fully satisfied with the legal services provided to me by Mark Brayford Q. C. and Hugh M. Harradence."

In his closing argument, Bob Hrycan brought up the issue of manslaughter once again.

> In the difficult circumstances of this case, we submit that defence counsel should not have rejected a manslaughter verdict as of no benefit to the appellant. Such a verdict carries no mandatory minimum parole eligibility. The appellant may have been convicted of two manslaughters and sentenced to life in prison. Such a sentence would not bind the parole board's hands in terms of a potential release at a future date. Defence counsel must have believed the prospects of an acquittal were better than the prospects of parole. A conviction for manslaughter with unrestricted parole eligibility was simply the best the appellant could hope for, and the trial should have proceeded on that footing and that footing alone. Defence counsel set about trying to secure an acquittal at the outset of the retainer. This was an impossible task, given the appellant's failure to explain his admissions, and should not have been attempted.

The three Appeal Court justices took a few minutes to ponder the issues that had been raised over three hours of testimony. After a fifteen-minute adjournment, Mr. Justice Tallis reported:

> We are all of one mind on this particular matter. The issue on this appeal is narrowed down to this, the

appellant seeks to adduce "fresh" evidence—and I put "fresh" in quotation marks—of incompetence on the part of trial counsel. Such incompetence has not been demonstrated. We find no merit in the appellant's complaint. Accordingly, the appeal must stand dismissed, since this is the only ground of appeal advanced before the court.

Two years after appearing before the Saskatchewan Court of Appeal and having his argument tossed out in short order by the three Appeal Court judges, Bob Hrycan remains steadfast in his belief that John Martin Crawford deserved a more favourable result from his trial and that his defence team didn't adequately represent him.

The basic argument—that Mark Brayford and Hugh Harradence should have acted differently to serve the best interests of their client—was a difficult one to advance before the Court of Appeal, Hrycan acknowledges, but he believes it was an important point that had far-reaching legal ramifications.

"Courts of Appeal are generally reluctant to receive an argument like that because there are some obvious professional differences of opinion that apply. Generally the courts have granted wide latitude to defence counsels in terms of the strategy they employ or the tactics they choose to use, what they choose to do, and what they choose to leave undone," he suggests. "It was an interesting appeal to argue in terms of legal issues, not necessarily with regards to the competence issue. You had a real serious dispute over what were defence counsel's obligations. It was equivalent, in my view, to the Ken Murray decision," Hrycan says, in reference to the Ontario lawyer who in the course of representing Paul Bernardo was accused of withholding evidence from the Crown. It was a charge Murray beat but not before a prolonged discussion of lawyers' responsibilities and duties. The Crawford appeal, says Hrycan, gave the court an opportunity to provide some guidelines on the issue, and, he suggests, "They didn't take the opportunity to do that."

Ironically, the appeal served not only to affirm the reputations of Mark Brayford and Hugh Harradence, but it also exposed appalling details of the crimes John Martin Crawford had committed. The revelations came in the form of an affidavit Crawford had prepared for the appeal. Methodically, he described the killings of Eva Taysup, Calinda Waterhen, and Shelley Napope, beginning with Eva, whom he believes he murdered around September 20, 1992:

> The day before the woman died, I had been using Ritalin and Talwin. I had injected it intravenously about seven times and consumed a couple of marijuana joints. I did not sniff any glue. I had "come down" from this high by the beginning of the day I met this woman.
>
> On the day of this woman's death, starting at 10:00 AM, I consumed two beer, one marijuana joint, two Valiums, two more beer, one joint, several more beer, some rum, more beer and approximately two more Valium by about midnight.
>
> I met this woman at the Barry Hotel at about midnight. I did not know her previously. I found her attractive. I began to talk with her and share a beer with her. She told me she was a prostitute and asked if I would like to go out on a date with her. We purchased a case of beer from the off-sale at the hotel and drove to the "cement pond." Here we had beer, marijuana and Valium. We had sex. She and I both wanted it. I was on top. She had nice big breasts. Afterwards we sat in the back seat and drank beer and smoked cigarettes. We were naked. We then talked about having sex again, drank more beer and smoked some marijuana. At this time it was about 1:00 AM.
>
> I then asked her to perform oral sex on me and she did. I obtained an erection and we had sex and smoked a marijuana joint while we had sex. She was on top. I had difficulty ejaculating because of

the effects of the marijuana. I ejaculated after about half an hour. She complained because this made her work hard. We put on our clothes again. The time was about 3:00 AM.

The woman and I smoked marijuana and had some more beer. I took the last four of my Valium. I suggested we get some food at the 7-Eleven. We had pizza pops and chocolate milk. The time was about 4:00 AM. I suggested having sex again and she agreed. We returned to the cement pond where we drank rum and coke and had sex again. I was on top and ejaculated rapidly. She was happy that the sex had not taken too long. At this time it was about 5:00 and starting to get light out. She asked me to drive her back [downtown] and then asked me for $150 as the cost for the three sexual acts. I became upset. I thought $50 would be appropriate and thought the last two sexual acts should be free considering that I had supplied all the alcohol. I refused to pay her the $150 and she threatened that she would "yell rape."

I recall grabbing her by the throat and holding on. I remember just holding on to her because I didn't want to go to jail. I remember her hands on my arms trying to get me loose and her stomach moving up and down. I remember thinking, "She's only worth $50, I'm not going to jail. She has no right to live." I remember realizing she was dead when she went limp but I continued to keep my hands on her throat for a while to make sure that she was dead. At first I just wanted to shut her up and scare her but I did not know my own strength. I was not trying to kill her initially although I did at some point realize she was dead. I slapped her face a couple of times after I removed my hands from her throat. I knew that she was dead and that the authorities would regard this as a murder even though I did not intend to kill her. I remember thinking, "Oh shit, nailed for another murder."

I put her body in the trunk of the car and drove about ten miles out of town. I had originally intended to cut her up. I used a saw to remove her lower left arm but decided not to because it took too much time. I tied her up in a blanket, wrapped the blanket with an extension cord, dug a hole, put the body in the hole and covered it up. I returned home, cleaned off the saw, and put it in the garage and went to sleep. I woke up about 6:00 PM that day.

Crawford's account of the killing of Calinda Waterhen follows a similar theme: the consumption of massive quantities of drugs and alcohol, sex at the cement pond, and eventually a demand for payment from the victim. According to Crawford, the murder likely occurred the night after Eva Taysup's death:

She asked for some money and I gave her $45. I told her that was all I had. She told me that her fee for these acts was $100. I became angry and said "fuck that" and she threatened to tell the police that I had kidnapped her.

I began choking her. I tried to stop her from talking and wondered how she could continue to talk. She kept saying some things about telling the police and I increased the force of my hands on her throat. All of a sudden she stopped saying anything and she was dead. I did not intend to kill her. I choked her to scare her. When she kept talking about the police I felt I needed to keep holding her by the throat. I was aware of the danger of death from choking from the previous night's incident. I relaxed my hands on a couple of occasions but she repeated her threats so I applied force to her neck until she stopped moving. After she was dead,

I remember thinking "fuck, here goes another one," but I did not think about performing CPR because I felt she was dead and there was no point. I was relieved she wouldn't be able to allege rape to the police. I felt bad about what had happened. I put her body in the trunk of the car and drove to the same place where I had driven the previous night. I removed the clothing from the body and covered it up with leaves and branches. I returned home and gave the car to my mother for her to use.

I felt bad after these deaths. I was depressed for about six months and didn't go out with prostitutes any more. I remember trying to scare the women and not kill them. Afterwards I thought that maybe I did it because I didn't want to go back to jail. I believe their deaths were an accident.

The affidavit conflicts with Bill Corrigan's testimony at the trial as well as statements Crawford himself made during his taped conversations with Corrigan. Again, liquor and drugs were involved, but this time Crawford described sniffing lacquer thinner with Shelley: "I remember thinking it would be nice to have a girl to sniff with but realized that would be a bad idea because I tend to get into fights with people when I sniff."

Crawford describes Corrigan unsuccessfully attempting to have sex with Shelley in the car, and then the two of them heading off into the bush:

About forty-five minutes later Corrigan came back with an empty beer and got something out of his clothes. I remember lighting his cigarette. After I had lit his cigarette Corrigan stated that "you won't have to worry about her anymore, she wanted $200 so I stabbed her and cut her throat." He told me this because I had told him before that I would not pay for his girls if they charged too much.

I asked Corrigan to show me what he had done.

We walked into the bush where I saw the girl laying on the ground with a gash across her throat, naked with no other wounds, laying on her back. I asked Corrigan for his knife and I then used it to stab the woman approximately eighteen times in the chest area to see if she was dead. I wondered if she was just playing dead. I was also angry that she had tried to get extra money from my friend. I remember stabbing her once and seeing no blood. I couldn't understand why there was no blood so I kept stabbing her to see what would happen.

Corrigan killed the girl. I did not.

"I would have told the jury what I have said in this affidavit," Crawford concluded, "if my lawyers thought it could have helped me."

With the thirty-eight-year-old John Crawford confined to the Saskatchewan Penitentiary at Prince Albert, serving three concurrent life sentences with no chance of parole for another two decades, and little chance for release in the faint-hope clause, the serial murderer seems destined to live out his life behind bars. But Bob Hrycan isn't convinced the situation for John Crawford is entirely hopeless. "I think that if William Corrigan was at some point to come forward or state in an unguarded moment what actually happened regarding Shelley Napope's death, then there might be grounds to revisit the issue."

There are questions that may never be answered.

Chapter Seventeen

DID ANYBODY NOTICE?

*"I can't help wondering what kind of reaction
there would be if these young women were
white. What kind of value do we place on
human life?"*

—Janice Acoose

Terry Hinz is one of the most respected Crown prosecutors in
Saskatchewan. He is also an astute observer of the media, perhaps as a result of having much of his work reported and scruti-
nized in print and electronic form. As such, he is well qualified
to analyze the media coverage of one of the highlights of his
twenty-five-year career: the trial of John Martin Crawford. As
the Crown attorney who successfully prosecuted Crawford for
the murders of Eva Taysup, Calinda Waterhen, and Shelley
Napope and put the sex killer behind bars for what will likely
be the rest of his life, Terry Hinz brings an insider's perspective
to the discussion.

"The media responds to victims they can empathize with," Hinz suggests.

That comment, succinct as it is, goes a long way in explaining why the murders of these three aboriginal women were largely overlooked by the national media and have now been forgotten by the local media in Saskatchewan. The Canadian public's awareness of this case is virtually nonexistent, even in Saskatoon where the crimes occurred. Ask anyone who John Martin Crawford is or who his victims were and you are likely to be greeted with a blank stare.

It has been almost a decade since Crawford murdered Shelley, Eva, and Calinda, and five years since his conviction for their murders—but the story is not over. The murder of Janet Sylvestre, the young woman who was well acquainted with Crawford, remains unsolved. And there have been no leads in the mysterious disappearances of Shirley Lonethunder and Cynthia Baldhead. Are the police working on these files? Is anybody in the media inquiring about the Sylvestre investigation? Is the RCMP any closer to finding her killer after more than six years? The silences on these stories are troubling. The families of Janet Sylvestre, Shirley Lonethunder, and Cynthia Baldhead are left to suffer alone over the fate of their daughters.

John Crawford murdered three women in the most horrible fashion imaginable, at times raping, stabbing, strangling, and dismembering. A decade prior to killing these women, while still in his teens, he committed his first homicide on Mary Jane Serloin in Lethbridge. He is a sexual predator, with four killings on his résumé, perhaps more. To date, only child-killer Clifford Olson has been more deadly in the ranks of Canadian serial killers. Referring to the deaths of Eva, Calinda, and Shelley, Terry Hinz says, "Looking at it objectively, there is no reason why the Paul Bernardo case should have received more publicity than the John Martin Crawford case."

There are a number of reasons why Crawford and his victims have been consistently relegated to the back pages of Canadian newspapers, when the story has been deemed newsworthy at all. Race, geography, incompetence, and economics all play a role. There are no easy answers to explain Canadians' indifference to this case—then or now—but as a society we must ask ourselves the questions.

The Crawford case illustrates the failings of the Canadian media when it comes to accurately and fairly following a national story that should have generated front-page coverage across the country. Terry Hinz is right when he suggests that the media are most comfortable dealing with stories in which they can empathize with the central characters, whether as victims or perpetrators. Leslie Mahaffy and Kristen French were the quintessential girls next door when they were murdered by Paul Bernardo and his wife, Karla Homolka. Bernardo himself was an intriguing contradiction: a handsome, intelligent young man from the suburbs, a man with a bright future . . . and a predilection for rape and murder. To the media, he was irresistible. Not so John Martin Crawford, a lifetime loser few people could identify with. Likewise, his victims were not women with whom the largely white, middle-class media felt any commonality. These women have been portrayed—not always accurately—as prostitutes, women who chose to gamble with death by participating in this most hazardous of professions. The mainstream media, conservative and decidedly non-aboriginal in terms of working journalists, were unable to empathize with the perpetrator or the victims and their families. Such crimes happen "to other people."

At the time of Crawford's trial in late May 1996, Saskatoon was served by three English-language television stations and the CBC French channel, half a dozen AM and FM radio stations, and the daily newspaper, the *StarPhoenix*. As the trial opened, reporters from all media outlets were in attendance. They were joined by Sandra Cordon, a Canadian Press reporter based in Regina. *The Globe & Mail*'s David Roberts, who covers Saskatchewan from his base in Winnipeg, also took in portions of the trial. The national television networks—CBC, CTV, and Global—relied on their local affiliates to file stories. As the trial unfolded, it became obvious that there was little interest in the story outside Saskatoon.

The mainstream media, as both a mirror of society's values and the messenger that delivers the dispatches it senses the public is keen to receive, make a judgement based on what they deem important and worthy of space or air time. The writers and editors working there bring an inherent prejudice to the workplace, much of it rooted in ignorance. It doesn't help that there are few aboriginal journalists employed in Canadian newsrooms.

Nick Russell, who has worked for Canadian Press, the CBC, and a number of other media in both print and electronic newsrooms, and is now an instructor in journalistic ethics at the University of Victoria, says that reporters are not purposely seeking a negative angle when they approach stories about Native people: "By and large, journalists are not racist," he said in an interview, "and I think they're driven very much by some basic ideas of what news is and what their readers want to read. Readers want to read what is new, what's different, what's strange, what's bizarre. They don't want to read the ordinary."

As a *mooniyas*, or white, journalist working in newspaper and radio newsrooms in western Canada, I have had the opportunity to observe the treatment of stories and issues involving Native people firsthand for almost twenty-five years. Overt or not, the racism I have observed has often shocked me. Some critics perceive the Canadian media, overall, to be a left-leaning bastion of social activists and self-appointed opponents of big business, big government, and what is loosely referred to as "The Establishment," yet newsrooms can often have another "personality." While stories about the underprivileged members of society make fine fodder for the front page, it seems, in my experience, that few journalists can muster genuine empathy or even sympathy for the subjects of their reports. Nowhere is black humour more prevalent than among journalists. Calamity and despair are often mere inspiration for the darkest witticisms. Humour that is unacceptable in other environs is apropos in the newsroom. Inevitably, these attitudes invade their work. The victims of such attitudes are the usual suspects: religious and racial minorities, the poor, and even the disabled.

Racism in the media begins subtly. In Saskatoon, as is the case in most western Canadian cities, there are a handful of older, poorer neighbourhoods where crime is widespread, and where most violent crime takes place. These communities are also home to a higher than usual ratio of aboriginal people. When a violent incident occurs in one of these areas, editors and news directors—assuming the police have even told them of the event—make a basic evaluation: is it news? Generally, in these inner-city neighbourhoods, anything short of a murder or an assault on an elderly person or a child is not deemed newsworthy. In Saskatoon, if someone is beaten in an alley in Riversdale or Pleasant Hill, it isn't news; if a similar incident happens in upper-middle-class Silverwood Heights or Lakeview, it is.

"News is the abnormal," according to Russell, "and if it is normal for violence to happen in an inner-city area whether it is black, white, or purple people involved—then it is not as newsworthy as when violence happens in places where violence doesn't normally happen."

Russell's analysis, accurate though it may be, is disturbing. What of the people who live in these less-affluent areas? What are we saying when some editor arbitrarily decides that tragedies taking place in their neighbourhoods are not worth reporting? We are saying, in fact, that bad things only happen to people who deserve them. Only occasionally do the media make forays into these neighbourhoods to examine the issues behind the violence: the problems of poverty, alcohol and drug abuse, and family breakdown.

This injustice manifests itself in biased portrayals of women such as Eva, Calinda, and Shelley. Journalists seek out juicy quotes that carry sinister, unspoken messages. "Sometimes she would bring strangers home from the bar," was one such revelation. You can almost hear the tongues clucking and the heads shaking as readers absorb such comments. Was Eva Taysup the first young woman to bring a man home from a bar? Of course not. It occurs regularly in all sectors of society. But by exposing the imperfections in their lifestyles, the media assassinate the characters of the victims, rarely finding the positive aspects that are there if only they took the time to search for them.

Janice Acoose, a professor at the Saskatchewan Indian Federated College in Saskatoon, analyzed the media coverage in her 1995 book *Iskwewak: Neither Indian Princesses Nor Easy Squaws*. "Native women are seen as objects, not really human beings," said Acoose. She continued:

> I have waited in agonized and frustrated silence for some kind of expression of concern (perhaps even outrage) from members of the community, women's groups, or political organizations. To date, few, if any, have come forward and spoken to the nature of this heinous crime or the need to protect Indigenous women who were so obviously the targets of this murderer. And perhaps, most important, I waited for someone to come forward and respectfully acknowledge the lives of these four women. Their existence on this earth has not been respectfully eulogized in the press in the same way that other murder victims' lives have been. And while the Saskatoon *StarPhoenix* carried reports of interviews with family and friends of Shelley Napope, woefully little else was expressed through the media that acknowledged their existence as human beings who will be sadly missed by family and friends.

Hurtful and inaccurate images of Native women are perpetuated by media coverage of events such as the murders of Eva, Calinda, Shelley, and Janet, Acoose argued.

> Instead of thinking about these young women as individuals who had dreams, aspirations, hopes and people who loved them, we were encouraged to view them through stereotypical images. Rather

than representing them as human beings who were brutally murdered, the press referred to them as women who "frequented downtown bars" and who were part of the "downtown bar scene." I wonder if depicting Taysup, Napope, Waterhen, and Sylvestre as women who were supposedly part of a so-called sleazy downtown street lifestyle somehow justifies their deaths? I also can't help wondering what kind of reaction there would be if these young women were white. What kind of value do we place on human life?

The answer is obvious. The public, seeing through the eyes of the mainstream media, has a very different view of tragedies affecting white society. Canadians have rightfully come to share the grief carried by the families of Leslie Mahaffy and Kristen French. Likewise, our hearts went out to the family of Melanie Carpenter, who was killed in British Columbia by Fernand Edmond Auger, a convicted sex offender, in January 1995, the same month that John Crawford was arrested in Saskatoon. Carpenter's murder sparked national outrage and led to renewed calls for harsher treatment of dangerous offenders.

Indian leaders have complained long and loud about the coverage of aboriginal stories in the Canadian media. They suspect the media are only on the scene when there is something negative to report, a tragedy or a legal issue. Perry Bellegarde, Chief of the Federation of Saskatchewan Indian Nations, has spent much of his term lobbying for changes in the justice system. But he knows that any comprehensive overhaul of the system will have to be driven by pressure from all sectors of society, not just Indian people. A stumbling block is the image of Native people shared by the rest of society, much of which he believes is manufactured by the media. The Crawford case was another example of the media setting a different standard when it came to a significant story involving Native people, this time as victims. In the end, they became "just another dead Indian" to most of us. We may have thought the story sad, but after all, hadn't they brought it on themselves to some degree? What could we have done about it?

Nick Russell also blames cutbacks for the inadequate coverage of the murder of these women. Daily newspapers no longer have reporters working on the aboriginal beat. "Most of those beats have been closed down in the last few years," Russell observes, "not because it wasn't interesting, not because it wasn't important, but because the publishers were trying to save money and that was one way to do it. Right across the country, aboriginal coverage is poorer in Canadian newspapers than it was ten years ago because there are very few of those aboriginal reporters left, and Saskatoon is one example of that."

When mainstream reporters do arrive to cover tragedies in the Native community, says Russell, they are often met with hostility, and for good reason:

> There is a resistance to that type of coverage because they see the largely white press covering only the disasters, and not covering the good news. So, if there aren't any aboriginal reporters to cover the good news, then the desk editors and the police beat are only doing the knee-jerk journalism of what happened on the police blotter last night, and they're not making the much more intelligent, sensitive decisions about what's important to the aboriginal community and how that should be covered. Violence in the Native community should be reported, just as good news in the Native community should be reported. But the resources just aren't there.

Saskatoon's dominant media presence, the *StarPhoenix*, was among the Canadian newspapers to sustain massive staff cuts following the takeover by Conrad Black's Hollinger. The *LeaderPost*, Regina's daily paper, suffered the same fate, as more than 180 employees, almost a quarter of them journalists, were handed pink slips as Hollinger made a concerted effort to improve the bottom line of these and other newly acquired papers in the province. It is hard to argue that editorial quality did not suffer as a result. And although the circumstances were not as dramatic, it was much the same story for the province's electronic media outlets. Would the coverage of Crawford and his victims been more in-depth and analytical had the media had more resources?

As the Crawford trial unfolded, it became obvious that there was little interest in the story outside Saskatoon. "If it isn't Toronto, it doesn't matter," one Saskatoon television reporter complained. Certainly the geographic factor was at play in the coverage of John Crawford and his victims. On Tuesday, June 4, 1996, less than a week after Crawford had been convicted, *The Globe & Mail* ran a large front-page photo of Marcello Palma, a suspect in the killings of three Toronto prostitutes. That, the editors of Canada's self-proclaimed national newspaper had determined, was front-page news. A triple-murder case in Saskatchewan was relegated to the inside pages, if the story made the paper at all.

Other Canadian newspapers were equally unimpressed. The Calgary *Herald* gave the opening day of the trial four inches on page A17, below a much larger story and accompanying photograph about the alleged crimes in Abbotsford, British Columbia, by Terry Driver, who was making a brief court appearance simply to set another court date. Driver was charged with the killing of Tanya Smith, sixteen, and the attempted murder of her friend, Misty Cockerill, sixteen, in 1995.

The *StarPhoenix* assigned the Crawford trial to Donella Hoffman, an experienced and capable court reporter. Her well-crafted stories, longer than normal for the *StarPhoenix*, were consistently played on the front page, usually with large photos. At the conclusion of the trial, Hoffman and Jo Lynn Sheane teamed up to provide *StarPhoenix* readers with a well-researched and well-written four-page profile of Crawford and his three victims. It was one of the few times the local media made any attempt to talk to the families of Shelley, Calinda, and Eva, and to present the three as something other than promiscuous women who drank in downtown bars.

In January 1999, when John Martin Crawford went to the Saskatchewan Court of Appeal in an attempt to overturn his three murder convictions the media and the public largely ignored the event. Only one journalist, Barb Pacholik, the Regina *LeaderPost*'s excellent court reporter, was in court that day. Her story was picked up in Saskatoon by the *StarPhoenix* and carried on page three. Perhaps this appears normal to readers who don't particularly care who is writing the story or where it originated. But there was a time when newspapers, including the *StarPhoenix*, took pride in following "their" stories to their conclusion. They took ownership, in a sense, over important stories that began in their own backyard. For some reason the murder of three Saskatoon women didn't fall under that mandate.

A year later, when John Martin Crawford's application for leave to appeal to the Supreme Court of Canada was dismissed, the *StarPhoenix* missed the news entirely.

Crawford's preliminary hearing, which was held in the provincial courthouse in Saskatoon in the early summer of 1995, produced shocking revelations about the investigation into the deaths of Eva Taysup, Calinda Waterhen, and Shelley Napope. For the first time, reporters learned how the RCMP, despite consistent denials over a four-month period, had a suspect in sight all the time, and were far from "grasping for straws" as police told the *StarPhoenix* just hours before Crawford was arrested. There was also evidence that tied Crawford to various sexual assaults and connected him to the murder of Janet Sylvestre. But perhaps the most incredible revelation came when two RCMP witnesses described how their surveillance team was within metres of the car in which Crawford allegedly assaulted a young Native woman. Reporters listened in amazement to the details of the assault on Theresa Kematch and how she was later arrested and held in the RCMP cells overnight. Unable to report on this evidence because of the customary publication ban, the reporters shook their heads in disbelief, wondering why the officers had not done something to prevent this attack. Each of them should have made a note in his or her diary to return to this intriguing story once the trial was over. Unfortunately, it never happened.

The Canadian media is comprised of thousands of individuals—intelligent free-thinkers who have a splendid opportunity in their daily lives to make a difference in how their fellow Canadians view their country and its inhabitants. Ignorance and intransigence about aboriginal issues can breed only despair and violence.

What happened to Mary Jane, Shelley, Calinda, Eva, and Janet is the stuff of nightmares. It has not been easy to tell their stories. But as Canadians we have to ask ourselves "what is news?" And "who determines whom and what we care about?" The deaths, and the lives of these women, deserve more than our indifference.